Improving Value in Health Care

MEASURING QUALITY

OECD

ORGANISATION FOR ECONOMIC CO-OPERATION AND DEVELOPMENT

The OECD is a unique forum where governments work together to address the economic, social and environmental challenges of globalisation. The OECD is also at the forefront of efforts to understand and to help governments respond to new developments and concerns, such as corporate governance, the information economy and the challenges of an ageing population. The Organisation provides a setting where governments can compare policy experiences, seek answers to common problems, identify good practice and work to co-ordinate domestic and international policies.

The OECD member countries are: Australia, Austria, Belgium, Canada, Chile, the Czech Republic, Denmark, Finland, France, Germany, Greece, Hungary, Iceland, Ireland, Israel, Italy, Japan, Korea, Luxembourg, Mexico, the Netherlands, New Zealand, Norway, Poland, Portugal, the Slovak Republic, Slovenia, Spain, Sweden, Switzerland, Turkey, the United Kingdom and the United States. The European Commission takes part in the work of the OECD.

OECD Publishing disseminates widely the results of the Organisation's statistics gathering and research on economic, social and environmental issues, as well as the conventions, guidelines and standards agreed by its members.

This work is published on the responsibility of the Secretary-General of the OECD. The opinions expressed and arguments employed herein do not necessarily reflect the official views of the Organisation or of the governments of its member countries.

ISBN 978-92-64-09480-2 (print)
ISBN 978-92-64-09481-9 (PDF)

Series: OECD Health Policy Studies
ISSN 2074-3181 (print)
ISSN 2074-319X (online)

Also available in French: *Améliorer la performance des soins de santé : Comment mesurer leur qualité*

Photo credits: Cover © iStockphoto.com/Soren Pilman.

Corrigenda to OECD publications may be found on line at: *www.oecd.org/publishing/corrigenda*

Foreword

This report is about how to improve quality in health care – a vital objective for health systems everywhere. Quality in health care is multifaceted and has various perspectives. Every patient has a right to receive timely, safe and effective care. Patients also have a right to be informed about the care process and about its risk and benefits. Those who fund and manage health care have a duty to ensure that scarce health care resources are used judiciously and wisely for the greatest public good.

The drive to improve quality does not stem simply from the fact that it is the right thing to do. Increased public involvement and awareness have been accompanied by a series of landmark critiques on quality in health care. The larger role of ICTs in health care systems has also meant that information relating to quality is now more abundant. Added to this, cost pressures on health systems have increased dramatically and OECD countries now spend more on health than ever before. Poor-quality health care ruins people's lives or kills them (Institute of Medicine). It is also wasteful and expensive and results in squandered opportunities to treat those with the greatest need and least capital. As such, quality improvement in health care matters to the economy and to society.

But how is better quality in health care achieved? How do we ensure that the views and experience of those who use health services promote improvements in quality? How do we measure quality and what are the benefits of ensuring that quality improvement policies are adequately linked with other related policy imperatives?

Based on the experience of the OECD Health Care Quality Indicator Project, this report provides a template for policy makers and officials who are interested in improving the quality of their health care systems. The report does not advocate a "one-size-fits-all" approach to quality improvement; rather it points to certain key elements that make up effective quality improvement strategies – principally, the requirement to align health care quality standards with national and local information systems developments, and to ensure that national strategies and policies aimed at improving quality are linked to robust quality indicators.

Acknowledgements

This publication represents the ongoing work of the HCQI (Health Care Quality Indicators) Project since 2003. The Health Care Quality Indicators Project was guided by an expert group made up of representatives from OECD countries participating in the project. The authors would like to acknowledge the representatives from the countries who make up the HCQI Expert Group, all of whom have given generously of their time in providing input and guidance for this work. This work has been built upon early contributions from the Nordic Council and the Commonwealth Fund and receives the continued support of the European Union.

The OECD would like to acknowledge the contributions of many colleagues and collaborators who have endeavoured to make this report possible including Niek Klazinga (editor); Sandra Garcia-Armesto, Ian Brownwood, Jeremy Veillard, Soeren Mattke, Saskia Droesler, Patrick Romano, Ali Tawfik-Shukor, Gerrard Abi-Aad, Vladimir Stevanovic, Rie Fujisawa and Lihan Diana Wei for their contributions. Sincere appreciation goes out to Mark Pearson and Gaétan Lafortune for review and comments and to Daniel Garley and Marlène Mohier for preparing the document for publication.

Additional thanks and recognition go out to the experts from participating countries and organisations who valuably provided the illustrative case studies that were included to give examples of the use of quality indicators in improving health system performance including: the United Kingdom, the European Union, Korea, Belgium, Czech Republic, Japan and Denmark.

Table of Contents

Tables

Figures

Acronyms

AHRQ	US Agency for Healthcare Research and Quality
AQUA	Applied Quality Improvement and Research in Health Care
AMI	Acut myocardial infraction
CAD	Coronary artery disease
CHF	Congestive heart failure
CLAB	Central-line associated (infections)
CME	Continuous medical education
COLD	Chronic obstructive lung disease
COPD	Chronic obstructive pulmonary disease
CQC	Care Quality Commission
CRS	Cancer Reform Strategy (UK)
CT	Computerised tomography
DVT	Deep vein thrombosis
EC	European Commision
EFTA	European Free Trade Association
EHR	Electronic health records
EPR	Electronic patient record
ESQH	European Society for Quality in Health Care
EUROCARE	European cancer registry-based study on the survival and care of cancer patients
FCC-CER	Federal Co-ordinating Council for Comparative Effectiveness Research
GDP	Gross domestic product
GP	General practitioner
HCQI	OECD Health Care Quality Indicators Project
HIRA	Korean Health Insurance Review and Assessment Service
HPV	Human papillomavirus
HTA	Health technology assessment
IARC	WHO International Agency for Research on Cancer

ICD	International Classification of Diseases
ICSS	International Cancer Survival Standard
ICTs	Information and communication technologies
IOM	Institute of Medicine
IQWIG	German Institute for Quality and Efficiency in Health Care
ISQua	International Society of Quality in Health Care
MRI	Magnetic resonance imaging
NAEDI	National Awareness and Early Diagnosis Initiative (UK)
NHS	National health service
NICE	UK National Institute of Clinical Excellence
PE	Pulmonary embolism
PSI	Patient safety indicators
PTCA	Percutaneous transluminal coronary angioplasty
QOF	Quality and Outcomes Framework Project (UK)
UPI	Unique patient identifiers
WHO	World Health Organization

Executive summary

Health care quality cannot be taken for granted

There is overwhelming evidence, from many countries, that health care is often not delivered in accordance with scientifically set and commonly-agreed professional standards. The result is that poor quality and unsafe care harms tens of thousands of people every year, and scarce health care resources are squandered. The good news is that many countries, which differ enormously in the way that their health systems are structured, are improving the quality of health care. Measuring quality is a first and essential step to reaching that goal.

The increasing complexity of health care makes measuring quality even more important. Patients are older than ever before, and (partly as a result) an ever greater number of patients have more than one health problem simultaneously. Medical knowledge, the availability of evidence and new technologies have increased as well, so more complex treatments are possible compared to the past. Not only are medical problems and treatments more complicated, but so is the health system itself with patients often being cared for across multiple providers.

Measuring, monitoring and comparing the quality of care in a health system are three essential ingredients for quality-led governance of the health system. Ultimately the goal of health systems is to deliver health care that is effective, safe and responsive to patient needs.

The OECDs Health Care Quality Indicators (HCQI) Project has led the way in providing a conceptual framework and methodological basis to provide the required information on quality since it started in 2002. This report presents recent work on health care quality and provides country examples that illustrate how quality improvement is brought about in practice.

Chapter 1 of this report focuses on *why we need information on health care quality?* It illustrates how improving quality of care lies at the heart of most health policy initiatives such as improving the coordination of care to avoid problems occurring at the interface between different providers (integrated care, disease management, case-management). It also discusses whether there is an effective strategy to ensure that the root causes of illness and disease are avoided. Measuring quality of care and patient experience comprise critical information inputs to policies that try to improve the patient centeredness of health care systems – one of the central objectives of policy in many countries. Quality measures are needed to implement pay-for-performance schemes, as are increasingly being introduced in OECD countries, and are necessary for assessing the success or failure of other policies high on the health agenda, such as health technology assessment and the co-ordination of care.

Using examples such as avoidable hospital admissions and re-admission rates, survival rates for cancer and 30-day survival rates for patients admitted to a hospital with a heart attack or stroke, Chapter 2 addressees the question *what does existing data on health care quality show*? Quality indicators gathered by the OECD HCQI Project demonstrate the scale of the quality divide across OECD countries. The chapter also describes the conceptual and methodological challenges associated with capturing and measuring quality differences. Key conclusions are:

- Data on avoidable hospital admissions for asthma, Chronic Obstructive Pulmonary Disease (COPD), diabetes and Chronic heart Failure (CHF) illustrate the importance of a well-functioning primary care system.

- Data on hospital case-fatality rates for heart attack and stroke show that there has been a huge improvement in quality of care over time, but some countries lag behind the best performers.

- Data on differences in hospital re-admission rates for schizophrenia and bipolar disorder between countries raise questions about the quality of mental health care.

- Data on patient safety indicators, such as foreign bodies left after procedure, accidental puncture or lacerations, and obstetric trauma in deliveries with and without instruments signal important questions about both whether reporting of incidents is adequate and whether policies to improve safety could not be improved.

- Data on cancer survival and mortality illustrate improvements over time but also that large inter-country differences persist.

The methodological challenges of international measurement of patient experiences are discussed, leading to an elaboration of some basic principles when setting up a national system for measuring such experience.

Chapter 3 tackles the issue of data acquisition. How can we get more and better data to measure quality? Data to measure quality come from various sources: death registries, disease registries, administrative data-bases, electronic health records and patient- and population surveys. Work over the past years has identified that the following technical and coding issues as being particularly important:

- The use of unique patient identifiers to link data-bases and thus monitor health care outcomes over time;

- Coding of secondary diagnosis and whether a certain condition (like an infection) is present at admission or acquired during hospital stay; and

- Whether data for quality indicators can actually be derived from electronic health records.

Addressing these issues is technically feasible; the challenge however is to introduce them whilst balancing concerns of privacy and data-protection. Quality governance and patient safety monitoring can only work when compatible privacy and data-protection regulations are in place.

Chapter 4 describes *how quality indicators can be used to improve health care quality*. An essential prerequisite to achieving this is to ensure that quality indicators relate meaningfully to quality-focussed policies. Collecting data at a national level which cannot be related to policies and actions at a local level – even by individual health providers – may have little impact on outcomes. On the other hand, if health providers can see that the quality of care they provide is measured, and see how it compares with other similar providers and more generally across the entire country (and even beyond), then they are likely to consider very seriously changes in practice which might improve their performance. In technical terms, the information that is collected to assess quality at the macro level should relate, where possible, to the quality information collected at the meso and micro level.

Conclusions and recommendations

Health care systems today face tremendous challenges – complex care needs and care processes, increased health care demands (especially for chronic conditions), and, fundamentally, an economic landscape where health care systems will have to achieve more for less. Measuring health care quality has a pivotal role to play in meeting these urgent and important challenges.

Poor quality care undermines every goal of modern health systems. It denies people potential health and at worst it kills them. Poor quality of care wastes precious health care resources – something that is unacceptable at any time, but even more so at the moment when money for health care is so tight.

In this report we describe why information on health care quality is important and how it can be used to improve health care. The report highlights examples drawn from around the world that illustrate how quality improvement initiatives can be implemented in real health system settings. Despite these examples, there is clearly much work to be done and quality improvements cannot be achieved with a 'one size fits all' solution. That said, the experience gained from international experts and quality initiatives in one country after another often point in the same directions. These are set out in the recommendations below:

Recommendations regarding the measurement of health care quality indicators

- Develop legislation that strikes a balance between privacy and data-protection and the need for reliable and valid information for quality-led governance.

- Exploit the potential of (national) registries and administrative databases for measuring quality of care- particularly through the implementation of unique patient identifiers, secondary diagnostic coding and present-on-admission flags (*i.e.* to facilitate the distinction between quality issues that are the responsibility of hospital or others).

- Implement the comprehensive use of electronic health records.

- Establish national systems to collect longitudinal information on patient experience.

Recommendations regarding the application of health care quality indicators

- Ensure that common quality indicators are used when considering quality improvement at macro, meso- and microlevels.

- Ensure consistency and linkage of quality measurement efforts with (national) quality policies on health system input (professionals, hospitals, technologies) health system design (distribution of responsibilities for quality and accountability), monitoring (standards, guidelines and information-infrastructure) and health system improvement (national quality and safety programs and quality incentives).

- Seek examples of good quality improvement practice from other countries, and identify how that learning can be applied locally.

Introduction

The quality of health care has become a major focus of efforts to improve the health care systems. Measuring quality is the first step towards improving quality and thus value in health care. This is not merely a national but also an international challenge. In response to this challenge the OECD Health Care Quality Indicator Project (HCQI) was launched in 2003 and has since developed and tested a range of internationally comparable health care quality indicators covering various health care domains. This report explains why information on quality of care is important and why it is central to effective health policy development. The report describes the indicators developed through the HCQI Project and the methodological challenges associated with their development. It also discusses how policies supporting the development of national information infrastructures can improve the measurement of quality of care. Finally, the report illustrates how quality indicators can be used to improve health care system performance.

The landmark report of the United States Institute of Medicine (IOM), *To Err is Human: Building a Safer Health System,* brought to light a worrying statistic: according to their estimates, medical errors probably killed more people than traffic accidents in the United States (Kohn and Donaldson, 2000). The 2000 IOM study was one in a sequence of studies over the past 40 years worldwide, showing the underuse, overuse, and misuse of many medical services. This growing body of knowledge questions common assumptions about the quality of health care. For example:

- Nordic data show that over 12% of hospitalised patients experience adverse events, 70% of which were preventable, over half of which lead to disability and increased length of stay (Soop *et al.*, 2009).

- An English study shows that over 40%, or nearly 1.9 million hospital emergency admissions, would have been avoidable if better primary care had been provided (Purdy *et al.*, 2009).

- Comparative studies, such as the Dartmouth Atlas of Health Care and the OECD Health at a Glance, show huge variations in health care quality within and between countries.

The result of poor quality of care is that everyone suffers: patients with their health; policy makers, for system failures and poor value for money; health care providers, with poor patient outcomes and job satisfaction.

Populations in industrialised countries are ageing, with an increasingly complex case mix of often chronic diseases, multiple co-morbidities and disabilities. Delivering care and evaluating its quality is ever more difficult. At the same time, increasing medical knowledge, new technological possibilities and fragmented care delivery systems make evaluation of the quality of health care processes and outcomes increasingly important.

In order to improve something, we need to measure it, and in order to measure something, an agreed definition is needed. Quality has been defined by the IOM as "the degree to which health services for individuals and populations increase the likelihood of desired health outcomes and are consistent with current professional knowledge". Most other definitions of quality are similar, often being expanded to include patient safety and also patient experience. Since its inception in 2003, the OECD Health Care Quality Indicators (HCQI) Project has focused in its work on quality on three domains: clinical effectiveness, patient safety, and patient experience (Mattke *et al.*, 2006).

As well as taking stock of the OECD's work on quality measurement, this report seeks to broaden the debate on quality measurement by discussing both the application of health care quality indicators and the national data developments that are necessary for their production. Four questions are addressed:

- Why do we need information on health care quality?

- What is the internationally comparable evidence on quality of care?

- How can we get more and better data, so that ministers, policy makers and practitioners are accountable and informed and so that they can learn from one another's experience?

- How should we use information on quality to improve health care?

Bibliography

Kohn, L. and M. Donaldson (2000), *To Err Is Human: Building a Safer Health System*, Institute of Medicine.

Mattke, S., A. Epstein *et al.* (2006), "The OECD Health Care Quality Indicators Project: History and Background", *International Journal for Quality in Health Care*, Vol. 18 Suppl. 1, pp. 1-4.

Purdy, S., T. Griffin, C. Salisbury and D. Sharp (2009), "Ambulatory Care Sensitive Conditions: Terminology and Disease Coding Need to Be More Specific to Aid Policy Makers and Clinicians", *Public Health*, Vol. 123, No. 2, pp. 169-173, Feb.

Soop, M., U. Fryksmark *et al.* (2009), "The Incidence of Adverse Events in Swedish Hospitals: A Retrospective Medical Record Review Study", *International Journal for Quality in Health Care*, Vol. 21, No. 4, pp. 285-291.

Chapter 1

Why Do We Need Information on Health Care Quality?

This chapter reviews why we need information on health care quality – to promote accountability, to inform policy development and to facilitate shared learning about quality improvement. The chapter also identifies key policies that have a bearing on quality-led governance and which rely on health care quality information.

Policy makers need to measure, evaluate and compare quality of care for three main reasons: to promote accountability among health providers, to inform focussed policy development, and to enable providers and other stakeholders to learn from one another (Veillard *et al.*, 2010). Indeed, there is now scarcely a policy initiative that does not seek to improve the quality of care, or that does not depend on being able to measure the quality of care. However, to achieve "quality-led governance", it is necessary to measure whether or not the system is delivering effective, safe and patient-centered care. The following policies depend heavily on health care quality information:

- Improving the coherence and co-ordination of care;

- Preventing illness and disease;

- Ensuring people receive care they need;

- Ensuring care is effective;

- Making sure care is safe;

- Rewarding health care providers for good quality care;

- The current shift of health care systems towards outcomes-based, quality-led governance.

1.1. Co-ordination of care

Interest in the co-ordination of care is increasing, with a focus on quality

Integrated care is becoming increasingly important and relevant in all OECD countries. It functions under a multitude of labels – Swiss managed care, English shared care, German Vernetzung or Dutch transmurale zorg, disease management, care management, managed care, and co-ordinated care – but all essentially seeking to achieve seamless, continuous and holistic care, tailored to the patient's needs (van der Linden *et al.*, 2001; Kodner and Spreeuwenberg, 2002). Therefore, it is a broad concept cutting across all health system governance levels and bringing together the disparate elements of the care journey – delivery, management and organisation of services related to diagnosis, treatment, care, rehabilitation and health promotion (Delnoij *et al.*, 2002).

This convergence of trends towards integrated care is explained by several universal developments. First, despite the differences between countries in morbidity and mortality of their populations, international health systems are confronted with roughly the same problems: namely those of ageing populations that have gradually entered the fourth stage of epidemiological transition. This is characterised by degenerative and chronic diseases that require different care delivery and organisational structures when compared with services for acute conditions. To summarise, the emphasis is shifting from acute interventions to monitoring, and from cure to care. Additionally, the optimal management of these types of conditions requires multidisciplinary teamwork, with patient care shifting from individual consultation to multi-professional teamwork, usually encompassing multiple care providers (Plochg and Klazinga, 2002).

Second, the pace at which medical technologies are diffused and implemented has led to more diverse diagnostic and treatment modalities, often straddling different providers and care settings – this multiplicity of care inputs also calls for more co-operation between hospitals and community services. In summary, patient care across OECD countries is increasingly characterised by multidisciplinary and "high-tech" care pathways with patients moving in and out of different settings. This implies that patient care will have to become more integrated at all levels (Dorr *et al.*, 2006). Thankfully, developments in information communication technology (ICT) can foster and facilitate ways of bridging health care silos, in ways unimaginable just twenty years ago (Mikalsen *et al.*, 2007; Gagnon *et al.*, 2009; Melby and Helleso, 2010).

Within this context, many reports suggest that the quality of care for the chronically ill can improve. Set within the context of tight public finances, a number of countries are now seeking to improve both the quality of care provided and to reduce cost pressures by streamlining the organisation of care with a particular focus on care co-ordination. A 2007 OECD questionnaire affirmed that most policy discussions about care co-ordination are most closely linked to goals of quality of care, followed by cost efficiency and, to a lesser degree, on ensuring access to care (Hofmarcher *et al.*, 2007).

The focus on quality is also highlighted by a wide body of research that demonstrates a longstanding and pervasive gap between current practice and best practice standards. For example, Asch (2006) estimates that half of patients in the United States do not receive the care they should, a result that echoes the report *Crossing the Quality Chasm* (Committee on Quality of Health Care in America, Institute of Medicine, 2001). Studies based on information from "root-cause" analysis of specific incidents suggest that poor design of health care delivery processes and fragmentation, rather than technical incompetence of professionals, underpins the majority of problems (Hofmarcher *et al.*, 2007; OECD, 2010b and 2010c).

In the next section, we show that integration and co-ordination of care is important not only within clinical health care delivery systems, but between settings of health and social care, and also between clinical care and countries' approaches to public health.

Targeted programmes appear to improve quality within health care, but evidence is inconclusive

Much policy attention has been focused in recent years on "targeted" programmes aimed at specific illness or population groups. These include, patient self-management, clinical follow-up, case management, multidisciplinary care and evidence-based approaches to change processes of care (for example, by using disease management or clinical pathways) (Ouwens *et al.*, 2009). These programmes are intended to increase the quality of care through various mechanisms, such as assigning specific management roles to professionals, ICT systems to monitor the care delivery process and facilitated patient self management. They also aim to reduce overall demand on the health care system by reducing unplanned hospital stays and the use of emergency services. In the main, such programmes were initially tried in the United States. Now they are widespread and appear under a multitude of configurations and labels among OECD countries.

Numerous studies have attempted to evaluate these programmes, but they largely draw on the United States experience. Current expert consensus suggests that such programmes appear to improve quality of care but are not always able to produce convincingly strong and consistent evidence. In addition, it is unclear which components or interventions should be included, and how such programmes can be implemented successfully. A study of integrated care programme reviews by Grol *et al.* (2006) found that care co-ordination improved outcomes. However, the impact on mortality remained unclear and little systematic analysis was performed on the cost-effectiveness of integrated care programmes. Only 15% of the effects reported in the reviews were significant and these came mainly from short-term evaluations (Ouwens *et al.*, 2005).

In addition, there are limitations in the scope of research and evaluation on the quality of integrated care. A more recent review (Grol *et al.*, 2009) found that there are currently no robust reviews of multidisciplinary integrated care interventions for cancer patients (Ouwens *et al.*, 2009). Their paper found only one study evaluating multidisciplinary care for patients with cancer. The study yielded very little insight into which interventions sustain the principles of integrated care, and what the overall quality and effectiveness impact was.

Quality of policies and strategies integrating health and social care

Integration of care becomes even more complex as patients – particularly those with mental health problems and disabilities – are forced to navigate between various care providers in a diversity of institutional and social settings (Zolnierek, 2008; Zunzunegui Pastor and Lazaro, 2008). All too often, patients fall between the "cracks" of different care settings. The root causes of these problems are typified by fragmented governance approaches in the financing, funding, organisation, management and delivery of care (Callaly and Fletcher, 2005). These issues manifest themselves in poor quality of care, increased costs, and ambiguous accountability processes.

Box 1.1. Policies and strategies integrating health and social care

In 2008 in England the new Health and Social Care Act came into operation. The Act introduced a new regulatory framework that covered both health and social care. It also created a new "super regulator" – the Care Quality Commission (CQC). The then Labour Government defined the new regulators role as "assuring safety and quality, performance assessment of commissioners and providers, and ensuring that regulation and inspection activity across health and adult social care is co-ordinated and managed". Since then previous attempts to build better links between health and social care have been strengthened. The new coalition government in the United Kingdom has introduced health reforms under its new White Paper "Equity and Excellence: Liberating the NHS". A key feature of these reforms includes the relocation of the responsibility for health improvement to local authorities. Local authorities are now also required to employ Directors of Public Health who will have responsibility for "health improvement funds allocated according to relative population health need". Quality measures are key to monitoring actual improvements.

Quality of care indicators are a necessary precondition for achieving better care co-ordination

Integrated care, particularly across health and social care settings is still relatively new and there is a pressing need to develop comparable measures of its quality both on process and its outcomes. However, the creation of such measures is complex for a number of reasons. Multidisciplinary professionals have different notions of what quality is; fragmentation in the development of information systems means that some sectors have better quality measurement systems than others and many of these are not interoperable. In addition, because health outcomes are difficult to measure and to attribute, accountability can become a sensitive issue (Lloyd and Wait, 2006).

Notwithstanding these significant challenges, it is feasible, at least at national and organisational level, to monitor the quality of integrated care. To compare the quality of integrated care cross-nationally, consistent and unambiguous definitions of the components of integrated care services must be developed (Ouwens *et al.*, 2005). In addition, better collection, analysis and dissemination of information on patients and provider performance is a cornerstone for building improved care co-ordination – interoperable ICT systems are at the heart of this (Blobel *et al.*, 2009). Valid and timely indicators are also a necessary precondition to facilitate policy development that enables multidisciplinary integrated care. Ultimately the goal here is to improve patient care by reducing fragmentation, improving accountability, patient involvement, transparency and quality of care.

1.2. Prevention

Advances in our understanding of health risk factors and effective interventions to prevent ill health have placed preventive care at the heart of health systems. Measuring and evaluating the quality of prevention strategies is important for several reasons: to garner an understanding of their mechanisms of action and potential benefits and risks; to measure their impact and appropriateness; and to monitor their relevance in terms of tackling health inequalities (Starfield *et al.*, 2008). Measuring the impact of prevention is also relevant because of the widespread use of expensive preventive technologies. These include, national cancer screening programmes, pharmaceutical preventive (*e.g.* the use of statins and oral hypoglycaemic drugs), policies that promote healthy lifestyles (health promotion) and public health protection.

Reviewing the evidence base on the efficacy of preventive modalities

Independent, organisations[1] now review and disseminate reports summarising the evidence for a wide range of preventive strategies (see Section 1.4). The recommendations that result from this research are relevant because they indicate which preventive strategies should be invested in. They indicate which population sub-groups they are appropriate and they evaluate their risks and benefits. Many of these organisations work in a multidisciplinary and transparent way, often working with national and international clinical experts, local authorities, and stakeholders from the public and private sectors, and even the community (Chalkidou, 2010).

Additionally, there is an increased focus on developing public health guidance with recommendations for populations and individuals on the quality of health promotion or preventive strategies. Such guidance may focus on a particular topic (*e.g.* alcohol), a population (*e.g.* the elderly), or a setting (*e.g.* schools) (Hashtroudi and Paterson, 2009; Kelly *et al.*, 2009). In the United Kingdom for example, NICE and the Centre for Public Health Excellence evaluate a wide range of public health programmes and interventions, covering topics such as obesity, mental health, smoking cessation, maternal health, sexually transmitted infections, and alcohol (Killoran and Taylor, 2009; Killoran and White, 2010). In the Netherlands, the

---

1. *E.g.* the US Preventive Services Task Force (USPSTF), the UK National Institute for Health and Clinical Excellence (NICE), and the Cochrane Collaboration and its affiliated organisations, such as the Nordic Cochrane Centre "Improving quality: integrating health promotion, disease prevention and health protection".

Rivm in its latest forecast report is also synthesizing the evidence on preventive interventions (van der Lucht and Polder, 2010).

Quality of preventive approaches – governance, policy and practice implications

Prevention now plays a central role in health system governance. Policy makers, providers, academics and patients actively seek and use guidance disseminated from organisations evaluating the quality of preventive strategies. Information gathered from these sources is used to inform a number of governance functions and purposes. These include, knowledge translation and transfer, policy development, setting quality standards, developing provider incentive schemes and accreditation programmes (see Section 1.7 on "Quality-led governance"), promoting quality improvement, and more recently, promoting international collaboration and cross-learning (Nicklin *et al.*, 2009; Chen *et al.*, 2010; Lester *et al.*, 2010; Morris *et al.*, 2010).

1.3. Patient-centered care

The Institute of Medicine's influential 2001 report, "Crossing the Quality Chasm", identified patient-centered care as one of the most important domains of quality (Institute of Medicine, 2001). The report identified several imperatives for achieving patient-centered care including the provision of better care co-ordination and integration, care information and education, guarantees covering the patient's physical comfort and emotional support, and guarantees to assure the patients physical comfort and adequate provision of emotional support for informal caregivers. Put plainly, orienting a health system around the preferences and needs of patients improves overall patient satisfaction and health outcomes, and even contributes to improved efficiency (Madhok, 2002).

The concept of patient-centered care has become one of the key characteristics of modern health care systems. Many countries have opted for primary care systems with a strong role for general practitioners in order to promote this goal (Landon *et al.*, 2010). More recently, "patient-centered medical homes" are one of the main health service delivery models being promoted by United States health care reform (Peskin, 2009). The model combines the core tenets of primary care with continuous quality and safety improvement, through the use of care planning, evidence-based medicine and clinical decision-support tools, and quality performance measurement, management and payment (Bechtel and Ness, 2010; Stange *et al.*, 2010).

If patient-centered care is to play such an important role in the management of health systems, then measuring patient experiences will have to become an essential component of health services evaluation. Many national and international surveys (*e.g.* Commonwealth Fund, Picker Institute Europe and US Consumer Assessment of Health care Providers and Systems) measure patient experiences, the results of which help drive accountability, strategy development and quality improvement (Quigley, 2008).

In Chapter 2 of the report (Section 2.7), we describe such initiatives, and outline some key principles for establishing national systems of patient experiences measurement.

1.4. Health technology assessment (HTA) and clinical evaluations

OECD countries currently spend trillions of dollars on health care, but have surprisingly little information about which treatment options work best for patients. In the absence of such information, millions of patients are put at risk, while significant portions of health care budgets are potentially spent on ineffective, unnecessary or even harmful care – the fact is that all health care interventions carry some risk (Subbe and Gemmell, 2010).

Health technology assessment (HTA) and clinical evaluation can inform health care decisions by providing evidence on the safety, benefits, risks and effectiveness of different treatments. These may include diagnostic testing, surgery, drugs, medical devices and even the organisation and management of health care services. For example, should aspirin be used for the primary prevention of cardiovascular disease? What age groups of women should be screened for breast cancer, and at what intervals? Are oral hypoglycaemic agents cost-effective, or even effective, for treatment of diabetes? Is screening for cervical cancer worthwhile, now that HPV vaccines have been developed?

To help answer such questions, many countries have established HTA organisations, such as the Danish Center for HTA, the German Institute for Quality and Efficiency in Health Care (IQWIG) and the Institute for Applied Quality Improvement and Research in Health Care (AQUA), the Canadian Agency for Drugs and Technologies in Health, the French Haute Autorité de Santé, and the UK National Institute of Clinical Excellence (NICE) (Bekkering and Kleijnen, 2008). The past 20 years have shown that HTA results are increasingly used for decisions on benefit packages and practice guidelines. Measuring the quality of care in practice, however, is key in establishing whether the rational assumptions made by HTA studies and practice guidelines live up to their promise in daily life (OECD, 2010b).

Linking quality and cost

Of vital importance in today's cash-tight economy is the contribution that HTA and clinical evaluation can make to macrocost control – this is especially the case for financing, policy, planning and regulatory governance (Temple, 2007). They are also the fundamental link between quality and cost – two dimensions often left un-reconciled, and treated separately by the research and policy community. It is for this reason that evaluation is central to current United States reform initiatives. Recently, The US government allocated USD 1.1 billion to establish a Federal Co-ordinating Council for Comparative Effectiveness Research (FCC-CER), to compare the effectiveness of thousands of medical treatments (Wilensky, 2009).

Box 1.2. EU co-operation on health technology assessment

In most EU member states, HTA plays a major part in evidence-based health decision making. The European Commission aims at enhancing the co-operation between the member states in this field.

To achieve this, the Commission is currently working on a joint initiative together with the member states in the field of HTA. This Joint Action aims to:

- Get clear orientations on what can be better achieved on HTA at EU level;

- Avoid duplication of work between national agencies;

- Spread expertise for the benefit of all EU countries;

- Strengthen evaluations carried out by EU countries;

- Develop transparent governance tools, notably vis-à-vis stakeholders;

- Produce a number of joint scientific assessments on interventions, medical devices and pharmaceuticals;

- Implement the EU Pharmaceutical Forum's recommendations on relative effectiveness of pharmaceuticals.

The Joint Action, set up for 2010 to 2012, involves 24 member states and the EFTA (European Free Trade Association) countries, Norway and Switzerland, and receives funding (50%) of EUR 6 million from the Health Programme.

Linking evidence on quality to policy and practice

OECD countries have come a long way in both producing and using knowledge and information to improve their health systems (Anderson *et al.*, 2008). Several countries have set up organisations specialised in developing effective ways of communicating research findings and evidence on quality of care. This is done under a series of labels and approaches – such as knowledge translation, transfer, brokering – but are all essentially aligned to similar themes of linking evidence to practice, in an effort to improve quality of care (Barer, 2005).

All these different approaches hinge on the same notion: only potentially effective care should be delivered. Quality indicators monitor whether this is realised in practice by assessing whether care processes are in accordance with medical science (practice guidelines) and what the actual outcomes are. Thus measuring quality of care is part and parcel of striving for improved effectiveness.

1.5.   Safety – the "quality chasm" persists

Perhaps no other subject underlines the importance of robust governance and quality monitoring mechanisms than increased public and professional awareness of the scale and breadth of medically-induced harm (iatrogenesis). As has been highlighted previously, it is in this area that a "quality chasm" has most evidently persisted. Historically, a lack of systematic quality monitoring mechanisms and proper regulatory processes meant that clinical errors could remain hidden. Today, with increased public awareness and involvement in health care processes, access to better and more comprehensive clinical data and an increased focus on patient safety, the tide is beginning to turn. Errors are more likely to be reported and actions taken to reduce their incidence.

A clear example of how these changes are taking place can be illustrated in the case of high rates of central-line associated (CLAB) infections. This form of medically-induced harm still persists in many hospitals despite the fact there is strong evidence that it is mostly preventable (Marra *et al.*, 2010; Tarricone *et al.*, 2010). In the United States, Leapfrog has partnered with Consumer Reports Health to release hospital infection rates for 926 hospitals at *www.consumerreportshealth.org*. The online infection rates reveal tremendous variations within the same cities and even the same health care systems.

Leapfrog has also published a list of hospitals that declined to report to the 2009 Leapfrog Hospital Survey, in an effort to "name and shame" non-participants. They are also urging consumers to find out if their hospital is reporting critical safety information. Central-line bloodstream infections cause at least 30% of the estimated 99 000 annual hospital infection-related deaths in the United States and account for USD 1.7 to USD 21.4 billion in avoidable health care costs. Safety programmes, such as the Keystone Project in Michigan, have shown that hospitals have the ability to reduce their central-line infection rates in ICUs to zero (Posa *et al.*, 2006; The Leapfrog Group, 2010).

Such initiatives are by no means limited to the US context. Since 2004, WHOs Global Alliance on Patient Safety has been delivering a number of programmes covering systemic and technical aspects to improve patient safety around the world. The primary focus of these initiatives has been to promote the development and use of quality indicators (Wilson and Walker, 2009; Weiser *et al.*, 2010). In Denmark, where reporting is mandatory, confidential and non-punitive, quality indicators reporting patient safety incidents have been published nationally for over five years. This initiative is at the heart of Denmark's continuous quality improvement programme (Hellebek and Marinakis, 2009; see Box 4.2).

Information on the quality of preventable adverse events has also been used in Sweden. One study in 2009 showed that over 12% of admissions had adverse events, 70% of which were preventable, and 55% of which led to impairment or disability and an increased average length of stay of six days. When these figures are applied to the 1.2 million annual admissions in Sweden, the results correspond to 105 000 preventable adverse events and 630 000 days of hospitalisation (Soop *et al.*, 2009).

These examples illustrate the importance of reliable, robust quality indicators; they also underline their pivotal role in preventing such tragic and costly events.

Chapter 2, Section 2.6, describes international efforts to understand the causes of medical errors and the development of typologies to categorise them. It also reports on progress with measuring, reporting, and implementing patient safety initiatives.

1.6. Pay for performance

Historically, most systems that have been used to compensate providers have not taken quality into account. In part this is because of an assumption that physicians do their best to provide good quality care. We also assume that hospitals do their best to create an environment conducive to treating injuries and curing disease. But evidence shows that a non-negligible proportion of clinical practice is of questionable value, in terms of quality and cost (see Section 1.4 above).

In all OECD countries, there are many schemes in primary care, hospital care and prevention that try to encourage the use of evidence-based protocols and incidentally decrease variation in health care. Pay-for-performance schemes go beyond encouragement and exhortation to reward providers to improve health care quality (Conrad and Perry, 2009). However, pay-for-performance indicators need to be integrated into a wider health system context, as it is important not to turn them into targets that encourage providers to neglect other important areas (Fink, 2008). The UK QOF Project (see Box 1.3) has shown the benefits of using a wide range of indicators, so as to avoid creating perverse incentives that would result from a narrow approach to health care quality. Although the scheme has not been thoroughly evaluated, there are some signs that the approach is improving the quality of care, along with achievements in reducing inequalities. Similar experiences are reported from Korea (see Box 1.4).

Box 1.3. Case study: the United Kingdom Quality and Outcomes Framework – a brief appraisal of its impact

The Quality and Outcomes Framework (QOF) is a UK-wide pay-for-performance initiative intended to drive up quality standards in primary care, and it has been a key element of the new contract for United Kingdom general practitioners since 2004 (Walker *et al.*, 2010). The scheme operates by rewarding general practitioners for achievement against 135 clinical and non-clinical indicators, categorised into four domains: *clinical* (e.g. coronary heart disease, stroke and diabetes mellitus); *organisational* (e.g. records and information; information for patients; education and training; practice management); *patient care experience* (e.g. length of consultations, access); and *additional services* (e.g. cervical screening and child health surveillance).

Performance against each indicator attracts points, and points attract money. In 2008/09 the proportional allocation of points was: clinical 65%; organisational 16.75%; patient experience 14.65%; and additional services 3.60%.

Although participation in the QOF scheme is voluntary, take up across the United Kingdom has been very high and in 2008/09, the proportion of the population covered by participating practices was estimated to be 99.7% (NHS, 2009). Average performance has been high from its inception with United Kingdom average performance exceeding 91% in the first year (2004/05). Expected performance levels, used by the Department of Heath for budget setting purposes, were estimated at 75%. The underestimation resulted in an over spend in the first two years of GBP 1.5 billion (NHS, 2008).

As a result of QOF's high cost, the over spend and adverse publicity relating to general practitioner salary increases, the actual cost-effectiveness of the scheme became controversial.

Evaluating the evidence on the cost-effectiveness of QOF

In April 2009 the Department of Health handed responsibility for development of the QOF to the National Institute for Health and Clinical Excellence (NICE). This change was seen as a need to sharpen the cost-effectiveness focus of the QOF and to redress the balance of reward from GP workload to patient-centered health outcomes (NHS, 2008). A number of high-quality studies have examined the cost-effectiveness of QOF. The table below provides a summary of the salient findings.

Summary – QOF, a good quality improvement scheme?

In conclusion, does this particular brand of pay for performance represent good value for money? Potentially yes, but high start-up costs and evidence that improvements compared with baseline trajectories have been marginal, probably mean that true value of the QOF are less than originally expected. Additionally, there is some evidence to suggest that GP productivity has actually fallen by around 2.5% in 2004 and 2005; this stands in contrast to the expected 1.5% increase in the Department's own business case on NHS productivity (ONS, 2008).

Box 1.3. Case study: the United Kingdom Quality and Outcomes Framework – a brief appraisal of its impact *(continued)*

Journal/Paper references	Main findings
Sutton, M. *et al.* (2010), "Record Rewards: The Effect of Targeted Quality Incentives on the Recording of Risk Factors by Primary Care Providers", *Health Economics*, Vol. 19, pp. 1-13.	• Recording of risk factors incentivised by QOF *vs.* non-incentivised risk factors, increased markedly (all risk factors investigated had similar pre-QOF trajectories) • The study also found a so-called "spill over" effect where other clinically effective risk factors not incentivised by QOF were also more likely to be recorded when compared with un-targeted patient risk factors
Gravelle, H. and M. Sutton (2008), "Doctor Behaviour Under a Pay-for-Performance Contract: Further Evidence from the Quality and Outcomes Framework", Centre for Health Economics Research Paper, No. 34, University of York, February.	• Average practice performance exceeded the threshold set for maximum payment of payment. On average practices could have reduced performance levels by around 12% without reducing their income • On average, QOF achievement levels were lower in practices with higher proportions of income-deprived and ethnic minority patients • Around 11% of the total number of patient exceptions may be inappropriate
University of York (2008), "The GMS Quality and Outcomes Framework: Are the QOF Indicators a Cost Effective Use of NHS Resources?", Centre for Health Economics, December.	• For QOF indicators where evidence on costs and benefits was available, all interventions under the 2004/05 QOF were shown to be cost-effective depending on baseline utilisation and change in baseline utilisation
University of East Anglia (2008), "Potential Population Health Gain of the Quality and Outcomes Framework", Report to the Department of Health.	• The study estimates that the clinical indicators set out in the 2006/07 revised GMS contract have the potential to save 452 lives per 100 000 in one year (reduced to 394 once exception reporting in 2006/07 is taken into account) • Over 50% of the total estimated number of lives • Saved stem from the coronary heart disease and diabetes QOF domains, however, the authors point out that there was significant baseline activity in primary care before the implementation of the QOF. The potential gains set out in the study do not describe the marginal benefits directly attributable to the QOF
Walker, S., A. Mason, K. Claxton, R. Cookson, E. Fenwick, R. Fleetcroft and M. Sculpher (2010), "Value for Money and the Quality and Outcomes Framework in Primary Care in the UK NHS", *British Journal of General Practice*, Vol. 60, No. 574, May.	• For nine out of over 100 indicators, QOF incentive payments are likely to be a cost-effective use of resources for a high proportion of GP practices, even if the QOF achieves only modest improvements in care. Although most indicators required only a fraction of a 1% change to be cost-effective, for some indicators improvements in performance of around 20% were needed. Only nine of the 100+ QOF indicators were considered in the study. The administrative costs of implementing and maintaining the QOF were not accounted for

---

Box 1.4. Korea's pay-for-performance approach

More than 99% of Korean hospitals and clinics use electronic data interchange processes and a unique patient identifier is in place. This has provided the infrastructure necessary for an innovative approach to improving the quality of care. The Health Insurance Review and Assessment Service (HIRA) of Korea is currently conducting quality assessments for 26 areas including acute myocardial infarction, stroke, coronary artery bypass graft, prophylactic antibiotic use for eight surgical procedures, haemo-dialysis, psychiatric hospitals, long-term care hospitals, eight surgical volume indicators, unnecessary C-section rate, hypertension and prescribing patterns. The publication of quality indicators based on these assessments has led to considerable improvements in quality of care and reduction in quality variations. In 2007, Korea went a step further and initiated an additional pay-for-performance demonstration programme. The new pay-for-performance scheme is called the HIRA-Value Incentive Programme (VIP). The scheme covers 43 tertiary hospitals and measures their performance in acute myocardial infarction treatment and unnecessary caesarean section rate. Thus far the programme has made a significant impact in terms of quality gains for AMI treatment. The C-section rate has fallen slightly. The economic impact has been estimated to be significant.

1.7.   Quality-led governance

As shown in the previous sections, measuring quality of care is now central to the development of effective policies aimed at improving the quality and cost-effectiveness of health care. Indeed, measuring and using quality of care indicators is now at the heart of most health policy decisions, heralding an era of quality-led governance. This represents a step change from previously fragmented approaches in the co-ordination of health promotion, risk prevention and health care provision.

Quality-led governance becomes a driving force in health system redesign, with quality indicators embedded in key governance functions relating to accountability, strategy development and mutual learning. However, to perform these functions correctly, particularly from a cross-national comparative perspective, some general principles on using quality indicators must be taken into account. Box 1.5 provides a summary of seven key principles to bear in mind.

**Box 1.5. Handle with care: seven principles to take into account
when using quality indicators**

Principle 1. Fit for purpose

The choice of quality measure should proceed from a clear definition of its intended purpose. Indicators designed with an external focus (*i.e.* oversight, accountability, identifying outliers, patient choice) will require different characteristics to those designed with an internal focus (*i.e.* quality improvement). For external use the quality measures should be sensitive to safety risks and signal changes over time, and they should be capable of showing meaningful differences between services. For internal use, more specific quality measures are necessary to monitor progress over time and to provide signals that offer clear and actionable management responses.

Principle 2. Clear signaling

Despite much progress, the validity of outcome measures is often debatable. Collecting information on outcomes like mortality and complications is useful but often it is hard to determine whether differences found are actually the result of differences in quality of care. For example, crude post-surgical hospital mortality rates have been used to measure whether a hospital delivers good or bad quality care. However, without statistical adjustment for complications and co-morbidities, differences between hospitals may not be due to differences in the quality of care provided. One hospital may only deal with straightforward, uncomplicated patients whereas others (such as specialist centres) may treat the most complicated cases.

Principle 3. Trustworthiness

The reliability of quality measures relates to the quality of the data on which they are based and the robustness of the method used to construct them. Reliability can be a concern where quality indicators are derived from databases that are only indirectly linked to the primary process of care delivery and data recording.

Principle 4. Beware of single indicators

Quality of care has different dimensions (effectiveness, safety, patient experiences) and one specific health care organisation (example. a hospital or GP practice) provides care via various processes involving many different professionals and technologies. Conclusions about *all* different quality aspects and *all* underlying services made on the basis of only one indicator are likely to be meaningless. Even a basket of indicators will have limitations. Organisational context and local knowledge of confounding circumstances must be taken into account when interpreting even well-constructed indicators.

Principle 5. A chain is only as strong as its weakest link

To avoid generalisation, attempts have been made to construct compound indicators that summarise the indications of a broader suite of underlying measures. Although this approach has certain attractions – simplicity and clarity –, the results can be misleading. Weaknesses of the underlying indicators are often disguised and the weighting between the various constituent indicators is often not based on empirical information or not reported at all. Thus the summary "score" can suggest a signal strength that is undermined by one or more of its constituent indicators.

Principle 6. A league table raises interest but is not always fair

The same methodological limitations that apply to constructing compound indicators also apply to league tables. Weaknesses in the underlying components may be masked, weighting is not necessarily user-based and ranking suggests real differences in the units being measured, *i.e.* hospitals, countries, etc. Additionally, without the presence of properly calculated confidence estimates, rank orders that imply absolute differences in quality, may in fact be nothing more significant than chance. League tables, especially those published through official channels, should therefore be handled with care.

Principle 7. Be aware of gaming and unintended consequences

Overall, reporting of information on quality of care can lead to performance improvement. Nevertheless, reporting on certain aspects of care can lead to adverse effects such as gaming or outright cheating. For example, reporting on hospital mortality rates has in the past led hospital professionals to try to improve their rates by promoting that patients die elsewhere. Furthermore, if indicators focus on major diseases like diabetes and chronic heart failure, this may lessen the interest in diseases that are less prominent in reporting and rewarding systems. Additionally, reporting on negative outcomes (safety, complications) should be balanced by reporting on positive outcomes (improved functioning, survival) – doing so will help to promote a balanced culture of risk control and risk taking in health care.

1.8. The cross-national character of quality-led governance

International comparisons of quality of care, such as those developed by the OECD Health Care Quality Indicator Project, meet a lot of interest from journalists and policy makers. Although the methodological challenges in providing comparative data are vast, the potential for cross-country learning is considerable. Given the epidemiological, economic, societal and technological demands on health care systems from all OECD countries, policy makers are looking for examples, benchmarks and solutions to address these pressures.

This increased interest in international comparisons of quality of care can be attributed to several factors. First, the public and the media are increasingly likely to hold policy makers accountable. International data therefore play a key role in the accountability agenda when countries can compare their relative performance to other countries. For example, negative user experiences of their health systems can lead to increased pressure on governments to seek out best practices and policy lessons from other settings (Schoen *et al.*, 2005).

Second, performance information from international comparisons, along with trend data and careful policy analysis, can form the input for national strategy development (Hsiao, 1992). Furthermore, by embedding strategic performance information from international comparisons of quality of care into decision-making processes, policy makers can assess and readjust strategies, plans, policies and related targets in order to improve performance (Veillard *et al.*, 2010).

Mutual learning constitutes the third function of international comparisons. Indeed, effective performance improvements based on performance data provided by the United Kingdom (Lomas, 2006) or Kaiser Permanente (Frølich *et al.*, 2008) or the Veterans Health Administration in the United States (Kerr and Fleming, 2007) provided other systems with an opportunity to learn from and emulate such efforts. As data get more robust, an analysis of the factors contributing to better performance becomes feasible and this knowledge constitutes an important part of the still limited evidence-based knowledge on health system quality engineering. With governments identifying peer groups against which to undertake such comparisons, the value in sharing similar challenges and experiences is greatly enhanced.

Linking performance measurement to performance management, translating performance information in meaningful ways for policy makers and investing in benchmarking and mutual learning are powerful policy instruments for governments to achieve superior health system performance. The OECD HCQI Project is a good example of comparative efforts moving in this direction. The scope of experiences is growing and covers comparisons at different levels of the health system and from different perspectives. The methodological difficulties can be addressed over time, but such exercises still require substantial investments of time and money.

1.9.   Strategy-based quality indicator benchmarking systems

Despite the methodological difficulties of comparative efforts, the diversity of benchmarking initiatives shows that there is great interest among the OECD countries to compare their performance and learn policy lessons from better performers. Selection of benchmarks is becoming more pragmatic and is increasingly driven by specific strategies to improve health care quality and performance expectations. Performance measurement then becomes the basis for policy discussions around how to improve health care quality and specifically about sharing what better performers have done to achieve higher performance in a particular context.

In this perspective, a well-designed benchmarking system has the potential to guide policy development and be used both prospectively and retrospectively (Nolte *et al.*, 2006). It can support better understanding of past performance and the rationale behind certain performance patterns (retrospective use) and also help revise strategies for improving future performance (prospective use).

The characteristics of such strategy-based quality indicator benchmarking systems are as follows:

- *Strategic focus*: the link between health system strategies and international benchmarking efforts ensures that policy lessons will be designed for those who can act upon the findings (the policy makers).

- *Adaptability and flexibility*: *benchmarking* efforts can undertake large studies (full health systems comparisons) but also narrower scope studies through tools that can be administered in a time-frame matching the agenda of policy makers (*e.g.* through patient survey comparisons).

- *Data standardisation*: efforts are made to standardise data and facilitate credible comparisons.

- *Policy focus rather than research focus*: benchmarking systems are not driven by experts or researchers but by policy makers with the support of experts and researchers.

- *Efforts to translate performance information and policy lessons for decision makers*: increasingly, new tools and approaches are used to convey data in a meaningful manner to policy makers while reducing the need to rank countries in league tables.

- *Sensitivity to political and contextual issues*: interpretation of indicator data should not lose sight of the policy context within which they are measured; of the players involved in formulating and implementing policy; of the time lag needed to assess the impact of different policies; and of aspects of health care that remain unmeasured by available data.

Cross-nationally comparable quality data are now often included in national performance reports, and are linked to national quality improvement initiatives and policies. For example, the 2008 Netherlands Health Care Performance Report benchmarks national performance using data from the OECD's Health Care Quality Indicators (HCQI) Project. As well as highlighting areas for potential improvement and learning, the report underlines the importance of quality as a driving force in regulated health care markets. The 2010 International Benchmarking of the Danish Hospital Sector Report used HCQI data to compare quality performance with a number of other OECD countries, and the OECD average. In its 2009/10 annual report, the England National Quality Board also compares its own performance on quality of care against various OECD Health Care Quality Indicators.

Chapter 4 will further address the question of how quality indicators can actively be used to improve system performance, by demonstrating how they can be linked to other national strategies to improve the quality of care. However before this discussion, the next chapter considers existing evidence on the quality of care across countries.

Bibliography

Anderson, S., P. Allen *et al.* (2008), "Asking the Right Questions: Scoping Studies in the Commissioning of Research on the Organisation and Delivery of Health Services", *Health Research Policy and Systems*, Vol. 6, No. 7.

Asch, S. (2006), "Who Is at Greatest Risk for Receiving Poor-quality Health Care?, *New England Journal of Medicine*, Vol. 354, No. 11, pp. 1147-1156.

Barer, M. (2005), "Evidence, Interests and Knowledge Translation: Reflections of an Unrepentant Zombie Chaser", *Healthcare Quarterly*, Vol. 8, No. 1, pp. 42, 46-53.

Bechtel, C. and D. Ness (2010), "If You Build It, Will They Come? Designing Truly Patient-centered Health Care", *Health Affairs (Millwood)*, Vol. 29, No. 5, pp. 914-920.

Bekkering, G. and J. Kleijnen (2008), "Procedures and Methods of Benefit Assessments for Medicines in Germany", *European Journal of Health Economics*, Vol. 9, Suppl. 1, pp. 5-29.

Blobel, B., D. Kalra *et al.* (2009), "The Role of Ontologies for Sustainable, Semantically Interoperable and Trustworthy EHR Solutions", *Studies in Health Technology and Informatics*, Vol. 150, pp. 953-957.

Callaly, T. and A. Fletcher (2005), "Providing Integrated Mental Health Services: A Policy and Management Perspective", *Australasian Psychiatry*, Vol. 13, No. 4, pp. 351-356.

Care Quality Commission (2009), "National Study Closing the Gap Tackling Cardiovascular Disease and Health Inequalities by Prescribing Statins and Stop Smoking Services".

Chalkidou, K. (2010), "The (Possible) Impact of Comparative Effectiveness Research on Pharmaceutical Industry Decision Making", *Clinical Pharmacology and Therapeutics*, Vol. 87, No. 3, pp. 264-266.

Chen, J., J. Tian *et al.* (2010), "The Effect of a PPO Pay-for-Performance Program on Patients with Diabetes", *American Journal of Managed Care*, Vol. 16, No. 1, pp. e11-e19.

Conrad, D. and L. Perry (2009), "Quality-based Financial Incentives in Health Care: Can We Improve Quality by Paying For It?", *Annual Review of Public Health*, Vol. 30, pp. 357-371.

Delnoij, D., N. Klazinga *et al.* (2002), "Integrated Care in an International Perspective", *International Journal of Integrated Care*, Vol. 2, p. e04.

Dorr, D., A. Wilcox *et al.* (2006), "Implementing a Multidisease Chronic Care Model in Primary Care Using People and Technology", *Disease Management*, Vol. 9, No. 1, pp. 1-15.

Fink, K. (2008), "Value-driven Health Care: Proceed with Caution", *Journal of the American Board of Family Medicine*, Vol. 21, No. 5, pp. 458-460.

Frølich, A., M. Schiøtz, M. Strandberg-Larsen, J. Hsu, A. Krasnik, F. Diderichsen *et al.* (2008), "A Retrospective Analysis of Health Systems in Denmark and Kaiser Permanente", *BMC Health Services Research*, Vol. 11, No. 8, p. 252.

Gagnon, M.L. *et al.* (2009), "Interventions for Promoting Information and Communication Technologies Adoption in Health Care Professionals", *Cochrane Database of Systematic Reviews*, Vol. 1, CD006093.

Grol, R. and C. van Weel (2009), "Getting a Grip on Guidelines: How to Make them More Relevant for Practice", *British Journal of General Practice*, Vol. 59, No. 562, pp. e143-e144.

Grol, R., P. Giesen and C. van Uden (2006), "After-hours Care in the United Kingdom, Denmark, and the Netherlands: New Models", *Health Affairs (Millwood)*, Vol. 25, No. 6, pp. 1733-1737.

Hashtroudi, A. and H. Paterson (2009), "Occupational Health Advice in NICE Guidelines", *Occupational Medicine (London)*, Vol. 59, No. 5, pp. 353-356.

Hellebek, A. and C. Marinakis (2009), "Decision Support to Avoid Medication Errors – How Far Have We Come in Denmark and What Are the Present Challenges", *Studies in Health Technology and Informatics*, Vol. 148, pp. 25-31.

Hofmarcher, M., H. Oxley and E. Rusticelli (2007), *Improved Health System Performance Through Better Care Co-ordination*, OECD Publishing, Paris.

Hsiao, W. (1992), "Comparing Health Care Systems: What Nations Can Learn from One Another", *Journal of Health Politics, Policy and Law*, Vol. 17, No. 4, pp. 613-636.

Institute of Medicine (2001), "Crossing the Quality Chasm: A New Health System for the 21st Century", Committee on Quality Health Care in America, National Academy of Sciences, Washington DC.

Kelly, M., E. Stewart *et al.* (2009), "A Conceptual Framework for Public Health: NICE's Emerging Approach", *Public Health*, Vol. 123, No. 1, pp. e14-e20.

Kerr, E. and B. Fleming (2007), "Making Performance Indicators Work: Experiences of US Veterans Health Administration", *British Medical Journal*, Vol. 335, No. 7627, pp. 971-973.

Killoran, A. and L. Taylor (2009), "NICE Public Health Guidance: What's New?", *Journal of Public Health (Oxford)*, Vol. 31, No. 2, pp. 296-297.

Killoran, A. and P. White (2010), "NICE Public Health Guidance", *Journal of Public Health (Oxford)*, Vol. 32, No. 1, pp. 136-137.

Kodner, D. and C. Spreeuwenberg (2002), "Integrated Care: Meaning, Logic, Applications, and Implications – A Discussion Paper", *International Journal of Integrated Care*, Vol. 2, p. e12.

Kringos, D., W. Boerma *et al.* (2010), "The Breadth of Primary Care: A Systematic Literature Review of Its Core Dimensions", *BMC Health Services Research*, Vol. 10, No. 65.

Landon, B., J. Gill *et al.* (2010), "Prospects for Rebuilding Primary Care Using the Patient-centered Medical Home", *Health Affairs (Millwood)*, Vol. 29, No. 5, pp. 827-834.

Lester, H., J. Schmittdiel *et al.* (2010), "The Impact of Removing Financial Incentives from Clinical Quality Indicators: Longitudinal Analysis of Four Kaiser Permanente Indicators", *British Medical Journal*, Vol. 340, c1898.

Lloyd, J. and S. Wait (2006), *Integrated Care: A Guide for Policy Makers*, Alliance for Health and the Future, London.

Lomas, J. (2006), "Commentary: Whose Views Count in Evidence Synthesis? And When Do They Count?", *Healthcare Policy*, Vol. 1, No. 2, pp. 55-57.

Madhok, R. (2002), "Crossing the Quality Chasm: Lessons from Health Care Quality Improvement Efforts in England", *Proceedings (Baylor University Medical Center)*, Vol. 15, No. 1, pp. 77-83.

Marra, A., R. Cal *et al.* (2010), "Impact of a Program to Prevent Central Line-associated Bloodstream Infection in the Zero Tolerance Era", *American Journal of Infection Control*, Vol. 38, No. 6, pp. 434-439.

Melby, L. and R. Helleso (2010), "Electronic Exchange of Discharge Summaries Between Hospital and Municipal Care from Health Personnel's Perspectives", *International Journal of Integrated Care*, Vol. 10, p. e039.

Mikalsen, M., S. Walderhaug *et al.* (2007), "Linkcare – Enabling Continuity of Care for the Chronically Ill Across Levels and Profession", *Studies in Health Technology and Informatics*, Vol. 129, Pt. 1, pp. 3-7.

Morris, A., T. Stewart *et al.* (2010), "Establishing an Antimicrobial Stewardship Program", *Healthcare Quarterly*, Vol. 13, No. 2, pp. 64-70.

NHS (2008), "Developing the Quality and Outcomes Framework: Proposals for a New Independent Process".

NHS (2009), "Quality and Outcomes Framework Achievement Data 2008/09", Health and Social Care Information Centre.

Nicklin, W., P. Greco *et al.* (2009), "Healthcare-associated Infections: Infection Prevention and Control Within the Accreditation Canada Qmentum Program", *Healthcare Papers*, Vol. 9, No. 3, pp. 26-31.

Nolte, E., C. Bain and M. McKee (2006), "Diabetes as a Tracer Condition in International Benchmarking of Health Systems", *Diabetes Care*, Vol. 29, No. 5, pp. 1007-1011.

OECD (2010a), *OECD Health Data*, OECD Publishing, Paris.

OECD (2010b), *Value for Money in Health Spending,* OECD Publishing, Paris.

OECD (2010c). "Health System Priorities When Money is Tight. Ministerial Background Note", OECD Publishing, Paris.

ONS – Office for National Statistics (2008), *Public Service Productivity: Health Care*.

Ouwens, M., M. Hulscher *et al.* (2009), "Implementation of Integrated Care for Patients with Cancer: A Systematic Review of Interventions and Effects", *International Journal for Quality in Health Care*, Vol. 21, No. 2, pp. 137-144.

Ouwens, M., H. Wollersheim *et al.* (2005), "Integrated Care Programmes for Chronically Ill Patients: A Review of Systematic Reviews", *International Journal for Quality in Health Care*, Vol. 17, No. 2, pp. 141-146.

Peskin, S. (2009), "How Patient-centered Medical Homes May Change U.S. Medicine", *Managed Care*, Vol. 18, No. 11, pp. 20-23, 28-29.

Plochg, T. and N. Klazinga (2002), "Community-based Integrated Care: Myth or Must?", *International Journal for Quality in Health Care*, Vol. 14, No. 2, pp. 91-101.

Posa, P., D. Harrison *et al.* (2006), "Elimination of Central Line-associated Bloodstream Infections: Application of the Evidence", *AACN Advanced Critical Care*, Vol. 17, No. 4, pp. 446-454.

Quigley, D.D. (2008), "Bridging from the Picker Hospital Survey to the CAHPS Hospital Survey", *Medical Care*, Vol. 46, No. 7, pp. 654-661.

Schoen, C., R. Osborn, P.T. Huynh, M. Doty, K. Zapert, J. Perugh *et al.* (2005), "Taking the Pulse of Health Care Systems: Experiences of Patients with Health Problems in Six Countries", *Health Affairs (Millwood)*, Suppl Web Exclusives: W5-509-25.

Soop, M., U. Fryksmark *et al.* (2009), "The Incidence of Adverse Events in Swedish Hospitals: A Retrospective Medical Record Review Study", *International Journal for Quality in Health Care*, Vol. 21, No. 4, pp. 285-291.

Stange, K., P. Nutting *et al.* (2010), "Defining and Measuring the Patient-centered Medical Home", *Journal of General Internal Medicine*, Vol. 25, No. 6, pp. 601-612.

Starfield, B., J. Hyde *et al.* (2008), "The Concept of Prevention: A Good Idea Gone Astray?", *Journal of Epidemiology and Community Health*, Vol. 62, No. 7, pp. 580-583.

Starfield, B., L. Shi *et al.* (2005), "Contribution of Primary Care to Health Systems and Health", *Milbank Quarterly*, Vol. 83, No. 3, pp. 457-502.

Subbe, C. and L. Gemmell (2010), "Numbers Needed to Hospitalize – Risks and Benefits of Admission in the New Decade", *European Journal of Internal Medicine*, Vol. 21, No. 3, pp. 233-235.

Tarricone, R., A. Torbica *et al.* (2010), "Hospital Costs of Central Line-associated Bloodstream Infections and Cost-effectiveness of Closed *vs.* Open Infusion Containers. The Case of Intensive Care Units in Italy", *Cost Effectiveness and Resource Allocation*, Vol. 8, No. 1, p. 8.

Temple, N. (2007), "Spiralling Medical Costs: Why Canada Needs NICE Medicine", *Healthcare Policy*, Vol. 3, No. 2, pp. 38-47.

The Leapfrog Group (2010), "The Leapfrog Hospital Survey", Retrieved 2010, from The Leapfrog Group at *www.leapfroggroup.org*.

van der Linden, B., C. Spreeuwenberg *et al.* (2001), "Integration of Care in the Netherlands: The Development of Transmural Care Since 1994", *Health Policy*, Vol. 55, No. 2, pp. 111-120.

van der Lucht, F. and J. Polder (2010), *Van gezond naar beter Kernrapport van de Volksgezondheid Toekomst Verkenning 2010*, RIVM, Den Haag.

Veillard, J., S. Garcia-Armesto *et al.* (2010), "International Health System Comparisons: From Measurement Challenge to Management Tool", in L.M.E. Smith (ed.), *Performance Measurement for Health System Improvement: Experiences, Challenges and Prospects.*

Walker, S., A. Mason *et al.* (2010), "Value for Money and the Quality and Outcomes Framework in Primary Care in the UK NHS", *British Journal of General Practice*, Vol. 60, No. 574, pp. 213-220.

Weiser, T., A. Haynes *et al.* (2010), "Effect of a 19-item Surgical Safety Checklist During Urgent Operations in a Global Patient Population", *Annals of Surgery*, Vol. 251, No. 5, pp. 976-980.

Wilensky, G. (2009), "The Policies and Politics of Creating a Comparative Clinical Effectiveness Research Center", *Health Affairs (Millwood)*, Vol. 28, No. 4, pp. w719-729.

Wilson, I. and I. Walker (2009), "The WHO Surgical Safety Checklist: The Evidence", *Journal of Perioperative Practice*, Vol. 19, No. 10, pp. 362-364.

Zolnierek, C. (2008), "Mental Health Policy and Integrated Care: Global Perspectives", *Journal of Psychiatric and Mental Health Nursing*, Vol. 15, No. 7, pp. 562-568.

Zunzunegui Pastor, M. and Y. Lazaro (2008), "Integration and Boundaries Between Health and Social Care", *SESPAS Report Gaceta Sanitaria*, Vol. 22, Suppl. 1, pp. 156-162.

Chapter 2

What Does Existing Data on Health Quality Show?

Using snapshots taken from the Health Care Quality Indicator Project, this chapter illustrates how health care quality information can be used to highlight quality variations, the conceptual and methodological challenges that arise when considering quality indicators, and finally the policy relevance of robust quality information.

There is now a wealth of information on health care quality in national studies. However, there is special merit in looking at comparisons of health quality in an internationally comparable way. International comparisons – if reliable – give countries benchmarks against which they can compare themselves. Potentially, such comparable information can also be used to assess why one country has a different quality of care compared with another. Thus far, such studies have been rare (see below for information on what is being done using OECD data on cancer survival rates). For now, the main objective of most comparative studies, including the OECD HCQI Project, has been to provide comparable, meaningful and timely cross-national data on the quality of care, focusing on effectiveness, patient experience and safety of care (Mattke *et al.*, 2006).

2.1.   OECD Health Care Quality Indicators (HCQI) Project: history and background

Systematic evidence about suboptimal quality of care and patient safety along with widely published incidents of poor practice have made quality a priority issue for policy makers. As a consequence, many countries have begun to introduce reforms to make health care predictably safer and more effective.

This increased interest has intensified efforts to develop quality indicators to assess performance at multiple levels of the health care system. But, while much progress has been made in tracking and reporting quality within countries, there is still limited data for comparisons across countries. This in turn has impeded policy makers' ability to benchmark the performance of their system against a peer group. Comparative research at an international level has therefore been confined to comparisons of cost and utilisation of care and health status indicators, such as mortality rates – the latter being more a measure of overall societal achievement rather than the performance of the medical sector. This leaves the broader question of value for money unanswered.

The Health Care Quality Indicators (HCQI) Project is attempting to bridge this gap. In only seven years, it has grown into a robust and sustainable effort to provide internationally comparable data on quality of care as well as a forum for policy makers and researchers to advance the quality measurement agenda. It now brings together a large number of OECD and non-OECD countries, international organisations including the World Health Organization (WHO) and the European Commission (EC), expert organisations such as the International Society of Quality in Health Care (ISQua) and the European Society for Quality in Health Care (ESQH), and several universities and research organisations.

Box 2.1. Countries participating in the OECD HCQI Project as of July 2010 (OECD member and non-member countries)

Australia, Austria, Belgium, Canada, Chile, the Czech Republic, Denmark, Estonia, Finland, France, Germany, Greece, Hungary, Iceland, Ireland, Israel, Italy, Japan, Korea, Latvia, Luxembourg, Mexico, the Netherlands, New Zealand, Norway, Poland, Portugal, Singapore, the Slovak Republic, Slovenia, Spain, Sweden, Switzerland, Turkey, the United Kingdom, the United States.

The project started in 2003. Inspired by two other initiatives by the Commonwealth Fund and Nordic Council of Ministers, a subset of 16 OECD countries started to collaborate on collecting a small set of "priority area" indicators for which comparable data were likely to be available (*e.g.* cancer survival and vaccination rates). After its early success and driven by the enthusiasm of its participants, the project progressed to a more systematic approach. This included the development of a conceptual framework to guide future indicator selection and prioritisation. The conceptual framework focused on the quality of health care, maintained a broader perspective of health and its determinants, and recognised the key aims of health policy (Arah *et al.*, 2006). It follows the IOM's description of the four functions of a health care system: staying healthy, getting better, living with illness or disability, and coping with the end of life, and discerns quality into dimensions of effectiveness, safety and responsiveness/patient centeredness.

Figure 2.1. Conceptual framework for the OECD HCQI Project

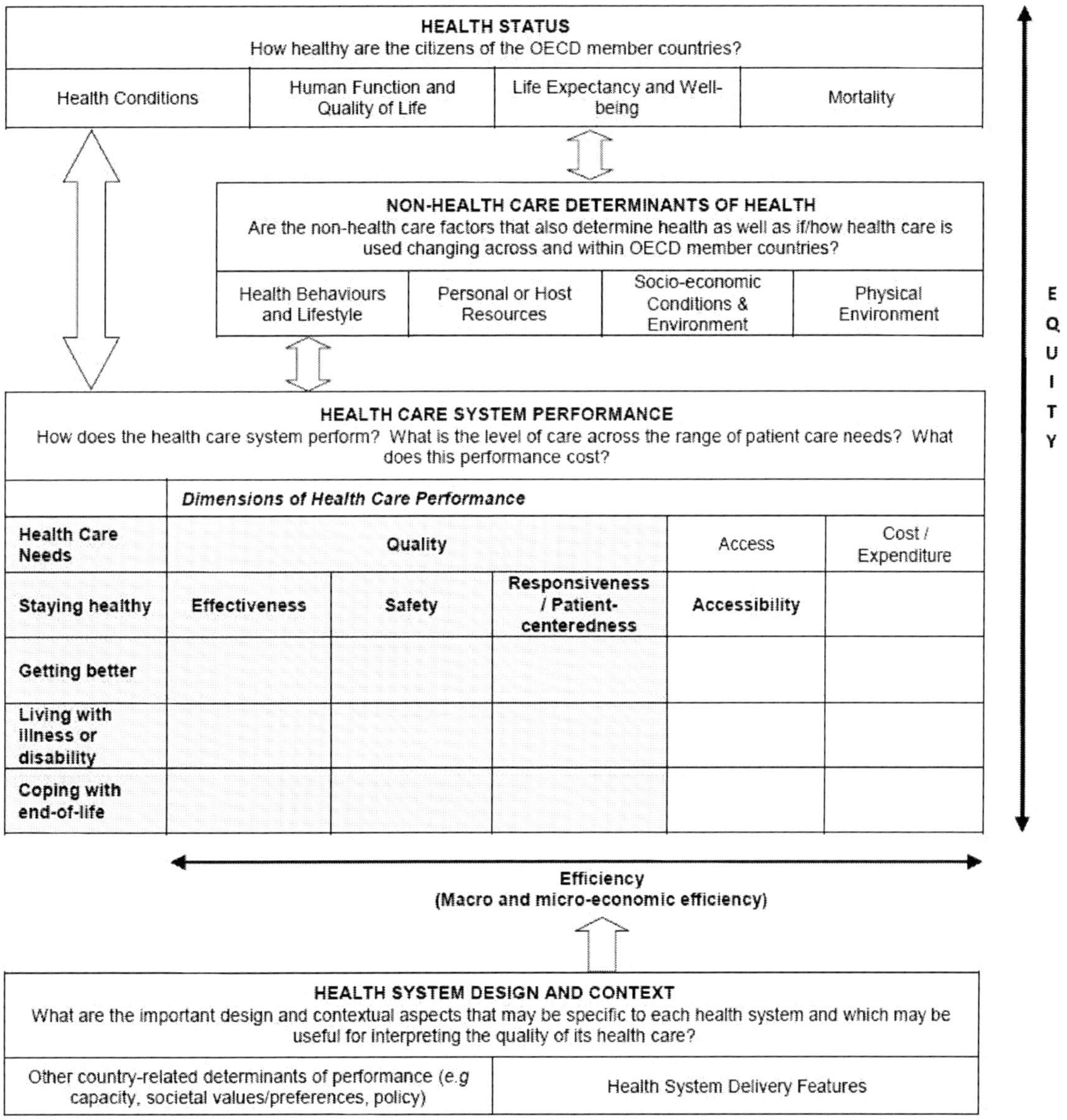

Guided by the conceptual framework, additional indicators have been added and research into data comparability issues has significantly improved the quality of the data. These efforts culminated in the publication of the indicators, first as a technical report in 2006 followed by *Health at a Glance* in 2007 and 2009. Subsequently, the project has focused on implementing a standard data collection process and quality assurance procedures. These procedures follow the successful model of *OECD Health Data*. The success of the project can be gauged from the fact that there are now nearly forty indicators that are routinely collected and reported every two years.

The HCQI Project has also been instrumental at informing the policy debate on health care information systems to improve the range and quality of data currently being collected. Currently, data are mostly compiled from administrative databases, registries and population surveys. Much effort has been invested into methodological improvements that include the assessment of data quality, refinement of technical specifications, enhanced data collection guidelines and questionnaires, and harmonisation of approach to age/sex standardisation.

The lack of health data infrastructures – in particular electronic health records, unique patient identifiers and database linkage technologies – is still the main limiting factor for indicator development. OECD work on information and communication technologies (OECD, 2010a) project provides advice in relation to the range of policy options, conditions and practices that can influence the implementation and adoption of ICTs.

Much work remains to be done until the project will have achieved its ultimate goal of providing usable information for evidence-based policy decisions. Many priority areas in health care are still not covered by the existing HCQI indicators, either because of data limitations or because of gaps in measurement science. Most indicators are only available for subsets of countries. And procedures to keep the indicators current in light of constant advances in medical science need to be established.

The following section provides snapshots of HCQI's work in areas such as primary care, acute care, mental health care, cancer care, patient safety and patient experience.

2.2. Primary care

Importance and relevance

Primary care has been shown to be effective both in preventing illness and death and, in contrast to specialist acute care, is associated with a more equitable distribution of health in populations. As such, primary care systems comprise the backbone of efficient and effective health systems (Starfield *et al.,* 2005; Kringos *et al.,* 2010).

Now, perhaps more than ever before, it is important to stress the primacy of monitoring quality improvements in primary care health systems. In its recent health strategy, "Together for Health: A Strategic Approach for the EU: 2008-2013", the European Commission identified "fostering good health in ageing" as a key strategic objective. In doing so, the strategy recognised the significant increase in the proportion of people aged 65 and over and the consequent demand on health care systems.

This increase in demand, coupled with a reduction in the working population, will significantly increase health care expenditure as a proportion of GDP. At the same time, EU Commission projections estimate that remaining healthy in old age can reduce the rise in health care expenditure on ageing by up to 50% – the saliency therefore, of primary care in mitigating and in managing the impact of chronic diseases cannot be underestimated.

The demographic shifts described above and the consequent epidemiological and health spending imperatives have heightened interest in primary care quality. In response to this, the OECD Health Care Quality Indicator (HCQI) Project designated the area of primary care, prevention and health promotion as a priority area for quality of care indicator selection and implementation. Additionally, the quality of chronic care was also addressed with a particular focus on diabetes and cardiac disease, two of the most common chronic diseases in industrialised countries.

In 2004, the OECD published the Health Technical Paper No. 16 "Selecting Indicators for the Quality of Health Promotion, Prevention and Primary Care at the Systems Level in OECD Countries" (Marshall *et al.*, 2006). The paper set out the deliberations of an expert panel in selecting a set of health promotion, prevention and primary care indicators with sufficient policy relevance and scientific soundness for consideration for international data collection.

The panel selected avoidable events to try and capture problems in the delivery of primary care, namely potentially preventable hospital admissions for conditions that are usually best managed in ambulatory settings.

Conceptual challenges

Designing indicators to measure quality in primary care is not easy. Primary care systems encompass a myriad of physician and nurse led activities and these straddle complex and changeable practice, community, social and acute care boundaries. Added to this, across OECD countries there are a wide variety of payment and contractual structures for primary care services.

Differences in provider payment and contractual schemes across countries can influence the scope of data collected and, consequently, our ability to measure the same thing consistently across health systems.

Despite these and other challenges, progress has been made in developing a suite of comparable quality indicators. Potentially preventable admission indicators are being used in a number of OECD countries. Although the indicators were developed through an evidence-based approach, there remain significant challenges in ensuring construct consistency across OECD countries.

Operational and methodological challenges

The availability of international measures of the quality of primary care systems is further hampered by the current state of primary care information systems – *i.e.* differences in both data coverage and data comprehensiveness. Although progress is being made in across a number of OECD countries, it still remains that the most robust source for deriving indicators on primary care quality is from routine hospital administrative data (*i.e.* potentially preventable admissions). These indicators have their merits in serving as a proxy for primary care quality but they are not direct measures of primary care quality.

Additionally, validation studies have been undertaken in a number of countries, many of which point towards the existence of potentially confounding supply-side and demand-side factors include age, sex, prevalence of disease and relative access and utilisation of hospital services. Previous OECD data collection on such indicators did not adequately consider potential confounding factors.

In 2008 the OECD specified a set of potentially preventable admission indicators for chronic conditions based on the AHRQ set of Prevention Indicators. Data was collected from OECD countries in early 2009 on these indicators, including supplementary data and information to allow for age and sex standardisation and consideration of other supply and demand side potential confounding factors.

Analysis of the correlation between cross national indicator values and the various potential confounders was undertaken. While some evidence of association was found, it was not strong or consistent across indicators. Sample size, data validity and temporal issues limited the scope of the analysis.

Other methodological issues were considered including the potential impact of variability of data coverage and completeness and specific indicators specification issues, including angina, asthma, COPD and lower extremity amputations.

Six potentially preventable admission indicators were presented in the 2009 edition of *Health at a Glance* (asthma, COPD, diabetes acute complications, diabetes lower extremity amputations, congestive heart failure, hypertension). Ongoing data collection, analysis and refinement of the indicators are proceeding. Additional national and international validation studies will further underpin the ongoing utility of these indicators.

Furthermore, in October 2007, the HCQI Expert Group endorsed a proposal to establish a Health Promotion, Prevention and Primary Care Subgroup of experts to assist the OECD in progressing related indicator development. To inform the initial deliberations of this subgroup a survey of information system and data availability was undertaken in early 2008 to assess the current and emerging capacity of participating countries to calculate relevant indicators.

The first part of the survey sought to assess the availability across OECD member countries of national information systems in the following priority areas:

- General practice;

- Obstetrics and midwifery;

- Women's, children and youth community health services;

- Home and community care for the elderly;

- Specific ambulatory care for chronic diseases;

- Pharmacies.

Table 2.1 provides a summary of the responses (E = existing and D = under development). Although further validation and follow up was indicated in order to more fully assess the level of utility of each information system for specific indicator calculations, the level of overall information system availability reported was encouraging, particularly in relation to general practice, obstetrics and midwifery and pharmacy information systems.

Table 2.1. Summary of information system availability by priority area

	Priority area						
	General practice	Obstetrics and midwifery	Women's children and youth CHS	Home and community care for elderly	Specific ambulatory care for chronic diseases	Pharmacies	Other
Australia	E	E		E		E	
Canada		E		D		D	D
Denmark	E	E	E	E	E	E	D
Finland	D	E	E	E	E	E	D
Netherlands	E	E	D	D		E	
New Zealand	E	E	D	E	E	E	D
Norway	E	E	E	E	E	E	
Portugal	E	E	E	E	E	E	D
Singapore	E	E	E		E		D
Slovak Republic	E	E	E	E	E	E	D
Sweden	E	E	E	D	E	E	D
Turkey	D	E	E			E	D
United Kingdom	E						
Existing (E)	10	12	8	7	8	10	
Development (D)	2		2	3		1	9
None reported	1	1	3	3	5	2	4
Total	13	13	13	13	13	13	13

A subsequent update on information system availability was undertaken in 2009. This review revealed that significant information system development is underway in many OECD countries, particularly in relation to the establishment of electronic health records for primary care and the interface with acute care.

The second part of the survey sought an indication from respondents of the availability of the set of indicators currently under consideration by the OECD, including a number of new indicators relating to the management of chronic diseases. The availability of the majority of these indicators had been previously assessed in 2005 and hence the responses in 2008 provided an opportunity to consider if data availability had improved or not over the three-year interim period.

The responses revealed that:

- Only 30% (17) of the indicators could either be currently collected or could be constructed from available data by at least 50% of the responding countries (cf. Table 2.2).

- There is no clear trend from a comparison of the responses in 2005 with those in 2008 that data availability for the 17 indicators has improved over the three-year period.

- Eleven of the 17 indicators had already been recommended for inclusion in the OECD data collections for 2008-09, including a set of nine potentially preventable admission indicators.

- Although availability had improved for 34% of the indicators assessed in 2005, only a few of these indicators were currently available in the majority of countries responding to the questionnaire.

Table 2.2. Indicator availability: at least 50% of countries either currently collect or can construct indicators

Indicator	2005				2008				Comments
	Yes	No	Total	%	Yes	No	Total	%o	
Physical activity	8	2	10	80	9	2	11	82	
Diabete prevalence	10	0	10	100	10	1	11	91	HCQI data collection 2008-09
Gonorrhoea chalmydia rates	8	2	10	80	7	4	11	64	
Abortion rates	10	1	11	91	10	1	11	91	
Congestive heart failure readmission rate	7	44	11	64	6	5	11	55	HCQI data collection 2008-09
First visit in first trimester	3	7	10	30	7	4	11	64	
Hospitalisation for ambulatory-care sensitive conditions	8	3	11	73	8	3	11	73	HCQI data collection 2008-09
- Hypertension admission rate	n.a.	n.a.	n.a.	n.a.	10	2	12	83	HCQI data collection 2008-09
- Diabetes admission rate	n.a.	n.a.	n.a.	n.a.	7	5	12	58	HCQI data collection 2008-09
Immunisable conditions	9	2	11	82	9	2	11	82	OECD Health Data
Adolescent immunisation	5	4	9	56	7	4	11	64	
Lower extremity amputation rate					7	3	10	70	HCQI data collection 2008-09
Cardiovascular mortality in patients with diabetes	5	6	11	45	5	5	10	50	
Avoidable hospitalisation for angina without procedures	n.a.	n.a.	n.a.	n.a.	6	3	9	67	HCQI data collection 2008-09
Avoidable hospitalisations for COPD	n.a.	n.a.	n.a.	n.a.	5	3	8	63	HCQI data collection 2008-09
Admission for uncontrolled diabetes	n.a.	n.a.	n.a.	n.a.	5	5	10	50	HCQI data collection 2008-09
Admissions for short-term diabetic complications	n.a.	n.a.	n.a.	n.a.	7	4	11	64	HCQI data collection 2008-09

The outcomes of this survey confirmed the relatively favourable availability of hospital administrative datasets and that they remain fertile ground for developing relevant indicators, including those relating to potentially preventable hospital admissions.

Findings and policy relevance

The indicators collected by the OECD on quality of primary care do not provide a complete assessment of health systems quality of care. Differences in data collection systems, definitions and methods remain. The underlying mechanisms that produce the between country performance variations are not fully understood. And more fundamentally, neither is the extent which the observed variation is a function of real quality of care differences or an artefact of the data quality?

In Figure 2.2, the 2007 normalised hospital admission rates for asthma, chronic obstructive pulmonary disease (COPD), diabetic acute complications and congestive heart failure (CHF) are presented. The graph provides a visual display of two things; between country variation in admissions rates and quality "distance" (the closer the lines are to the centre the lower the volume of potentially preventable admissions).

The graph shows that there are very significant variations in indicator values across the board and if these are measures of quality it also shows that some countries appear to do well in certain primary care areas but not in others.

Taking each of the conditions in turn, for asthma, the United States, Finland, Korea and to a lesser extent New Zealand all stand out as outliers with high admission rates for this condition. For COPD, Ireland, Austria, Denmark and New Zealand have relatively high values. For diabetic acute complications, the United States, Ireland and Finland also stand out. And finally for CHF, Poland, the United States, Germany and Italy all have high values.

Figure 2.2. Avoidable hospital admission rates, 2007

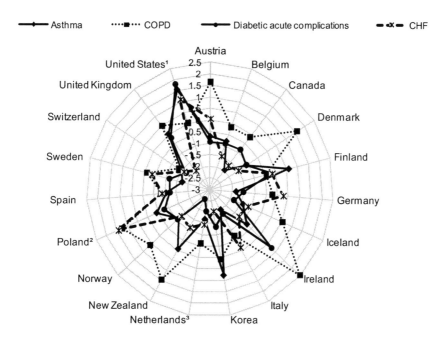

CHF = Congestive heart failure; COPD = Chronic obstructive pulmonary disease.

Note: The number of hospital admissions of people aged 15 years and over per 100 000 population, age and sex-standardised rates in relation to OECD average. Values have been normalised for ease of interpretation. Data from Austria, Belgium, Italy, Poland, Switzerland and the United States refer to 2006. Data from the Netherlands refer to 2005.

1. Data does not fully exclude day cases.

2. Data includes transfers from other hospitals and/or other units within the same hospitals, which marginally elevate the rates.

3. Data for CHF includes admissions for additional diagnosis codes, which marginally elevate the rate.

Source: OECD Health Care Quality Indicators Database, 2009.

Next steps

Further development work with respect to indicator development and interpretation of cross country variations is needed.

- The primary care information systems development survey referred to earlier revealed that there are significant developments taking place with respect to the implementation of electronic health records and record linkage capabilities. Future OECD work will explore and report on the potential of these developments with a view to exploiting quality indicators around joined up care.

- Work will continue to examine the potential confounding and explanatory factors, including opportunities to access comparable cross-national prevalence data.

- Further data on hospital coverage will be collected with a view to assessing the feasibility and merit of establishing an appropriate data adjustment methodology.

2.3. Acute care for chronic conditions using coronary artery disease (CAD) as an example

Importance and relevance

Acute hospital care has become a poster child for the advances and benefits of high-tech medicine. Improved imaging technologies and laboratory tests provide rapid and precise diagnoses, powerful drugs help stabilise patients and new surgical and interventional approaches save people's lives. Better processes of care make sure that these life-saving measures are used appropriately. The progress described exemplifies how research from a variety of disciplines can make medical care better and improve outcomes.

Acute cardiovascular events, such as stroke and acute myocardial infarction (AMI), are prime illustrations of the impact of medical progress. In AMI, a blood clot occludes one of the pencil-thin arteries that supply blood to the heart, leading to irreversible loss of cardiac function and potentially heart failure or cardiac arrest, if untreated. In stroke the same phenomena occurs in the brain (ischemic stroke) or bleeding occurs (hemorrhagic stroke).While coronary artery disease (CAD) still remains the leading cause of death in industrialised countries, CAD mortality rates have been in decline since the 1970s (Weisfeldt and Zieman, 2007). This success is all the more remarkable as data suggest that the incidence of AMI has not declined in parallel (Goldberg et al., 1999).

Much of the reduction in mortality can be attributed to lower acute mortality from AMI (Capewell et al., 1999; McGovern et al., 2001) due to better treatment in the acute phase. Care for AMI has changed dramatically in the last few decades, first with the introduction of coronary care units in the 1960s (Khush et al., 2005) and then with the advent of treatment aimed at restoring coronary blood flow in the 1980s (Gil, 1999). First, this was achieved by thrombolysis, i.e., administration of intravenous drugs that dissolve the blood clot, then by percutaneous coronary interventions, in which a catheter is advanced into the patients' coronary artery and the clot pushed away with an inflatable balloon. Cardiologists have also started to insert so-called coronary stents, tiny wire tubes that keep the artery from closing up again. Not just medical technology but also improved processes contributed to better outcomes: as research showed that the time from AMI to re-opening the artery was a key driver of prognosis, care processes were changed radically. Many drugs, such as aspirin and heparin, are now administered by emergency medical personnel during transport to hospital. Emergency departments have instituted procedures to ensure that patients receive definite treatment with thrombolysis or catheterisation within minutes of arrival.

Conceptual challenges

Advances in acute cardiovascular care were typically supported by large and rigorously designed clinical trials. This has resulted in the production of a comprehensive evidence base upon which effective care processes can be developed. These care processes also get codified into practice guidelines in which professional societies define the current standards of care. Thus, there is an evidence base that allows defining process quality indicators which capture the degree to which those widely accepted standards of care are followed. The proven link between those care processes and patient outcomes, such as survival and neurological deficit, also allow construction of outcomes quality indicators which reflect the end result of care.

Numerous indicators, in particular for AMI care, have been developed over the years and are widely accepted. For example, the case-fatality for AMI within 30 days was one of the first HCQI indicators selected and the initial report of the HCQI Subcommittee of Cardiac Care recommended four AMI indicators (timing of thrombolysis, timing of emergency PTCA, aspirin at admission to hospital and one year mortality).

Operational and methodological challenges

While conceptually the science of measuring quality of care for acute cardiovascular condition is well established, collecting comparable data for those indicators remains a challenge, especially on the international level. Many variables required to construct quality indicators, for example, the time between patient arrival and start of thrombolysis, are only documented in the patient's medical records. Few countries have ongoing national data collection and reporting initiatives for such variables. This means that the required data are typically only available in the context of local quality improvement or research projects.

However, data are available for a sufficient number of countries to include 30-day case-fatality rates for AMI, ischemic stroke and hemorrhagic stroke in the indicator set. But several methodological challenges remain as a result of data limitations. Ideally, one would track every patient for 30 days after the initial hospital admission to ascertain whether they survived or not. However, because most countries do not have unique patient identifiers this is not feasible. As a consequence, the indicators could only be implemented as 30-day case fatality rate within the hospital, i.e. it is implicitly assumed that all patients survived who were discharged before 30 days. This is not an ideal approach however, analyses form countries that do have linkage capabilities suggest that the error introduced by this modification is small. Another concern is the lack of information to adjust for differential patient risk profiles across countries.

Findings and policy relevance

Figure 2.3 shows crude and age- and sex-standardised in-hospital case-fatality rates within 30 days of admission for AMI. The average rate is 5.3%, but there is an up to fivefold difference between the highest rates (Japan 9.7%) and the lowest rates (Iceland 2.1%). A cluster of Nordic countries (i.e. Finland, Sweden, Norway, Denmark and Iceland) are well below the average rate. It should be noted, however, that differences in hospital transfers, average lengths of stay and emergency retrieval times, can influence reported rates. For example, some countries have a system of emergency care where physicians, who are specialists in advanced life support, retrieve critically ill patients alongside emergency medical technicians. As a result, more patients reach the hospital alive but ultimately cannot be stabilised and die shortly after admission. In other countries, unstable cardiac patients are commonly transferred to tertiary care centres, possibly biasing case-fatality rates downward, if the transfer is recorded as a live discharge.

Figure 2.3. In-hospital case-fatality rates within 30 days after admission for AMI, 2007

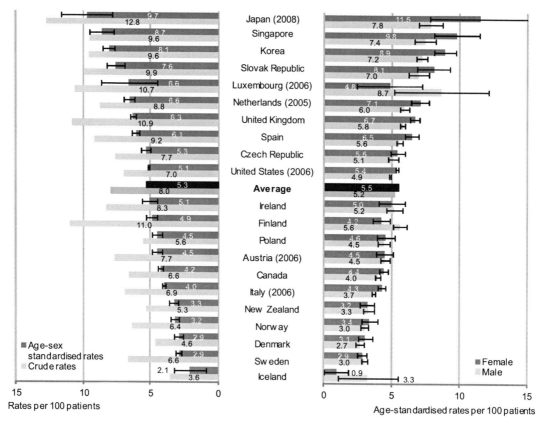

Note: Rates age-sex standardised to 2005 OECD population (45+). 95% confidence intervals represented by H. Rates from Japan refer to a one month sample.

Source: OECD Health Care Quality Indicators Database, 2009.

The right-hand side of the figure shows that AMI case-fatality rates are typically higher for women than for men, but the difference is typically not statistically significant. This likely reflects the fact that, while CAD is much more common in men than in women, it is usually more severe in women.

Figure 2.4 shows that case-fatality rates for AMI are decreasing over time in all reporting OECD countries, with the majority of the countries recording statistically significant reductions between 2001 and 2007. These substantial improvements reflect better and more reliable processes of care, in particular with respect to rapid re-opening of the occluded arteries. Research in many countries, such as Canada, has explicitly linked those process improvements to better survival rates (Fox *et al.*, 2007; Tu *et al.*, 2009).

Figure 2.4. Reduction in in-hospital case-fatality rates within 30 days after admission for AMI, 2003-07 (or nearest available year)

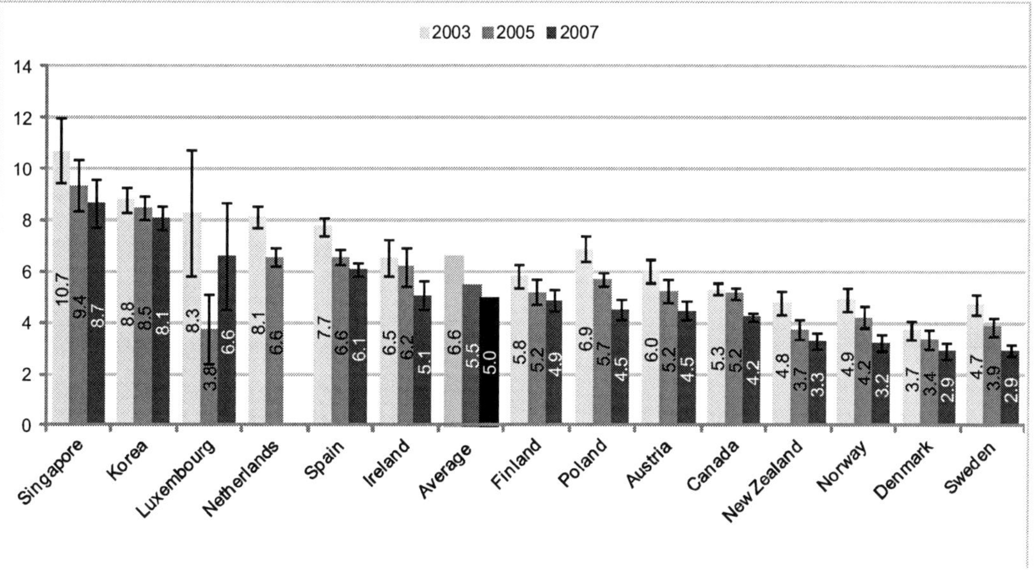

Note: Rates age-sex standardised to 2005 OECD population (45+). 95% confidence intervals represented by H.

Source: OECD Health Care Quality Indicators Database, 2009.

Progress, next steps and recommendations

The HCQI Project indicators for acute hospital care symbolise both the progress that the project has made in providing data for better policy decisions and, the work that remains. The results demonstrate continuous improvement in survival of patients with AMI and there are similar patterns of progress for stroke also. Differences in performance across OECD countries remain substantial. While it is not possible to rule out that some of these differences are caused by data issues rather than real variations in quality, the findings point to opportunities for cross-country health system learning to ensure that improvement potential is maximised. Better availability of comparable process indicators would facilitate this learning process, because these types of measures can provide information on how countries achieve their results.

2.4. Mental health

Importance and relevance

Mental health problems are common, affecting all sections of society and every age group. The WHO estimates that about 10% of the adult population worldwide will report having some type of mental or behavioural disorder at any point in time. Both US and European studies have found that over a quarter of adults are annually affected by at least one mental disorder (Garcia-Armesto *et al.*, 2008). Even though these disorders are widespread, the main burden occurs among a smaller proportion of the population suffering from serious mental illnesses, such as severe depression, schizophrenia, bipolar disorder, dementia or alcohol and drug dependence (Prince *et al.*, 2007; Eaton *et al.*, 2008; Fajutrao *et al.*, 2009).

The burden and cost of mental health disorders

The morbidity and mortality burden of mental health disorders is enormous. Almost all suicides are associated with a mental health disorder and these are commonly used as a measure of serious health problems in populations. In 2005, 140 000 people in OECD countries took their own lives, equating to 12 per 100 000 population, with huge – largely unexplained – variations in rates both between and within countries (Garcia-Armesto *et al.*, 2008).

Furthermore, the burden of living with mental health problems is enormous. Mental disorders are the leading cause of disability in the United States and Canada for ages 15-44, with many people suffering from multiple mental disorders simultaneously with severity strongly related to comorbidity. Mental disorders now account for up to 28% of global disability-adjusted life years (DALYs) – more than cardiovascular disease and cancer (Granados *et al.*, 2005; Rossler *et al.*, 2005; Kastrup and Ramos, 2007). However it is estimated that the real contribution of mental disorders to the global burden of disease is even higher, due to complex interactions and comorbidity of physical and mental illness.

The economic and social cost of mental health problems to society is also substantial (Knapp *et al.*, 2004). A conservative estimate from the International Labour Organisation put them at between 3% and 4% of GDP in the European Union. Studies on the cost of illnesses carried out in seven OECD countries during the past ten years show that care for mental and behavioural disorders accounted for 9% of total health care costs on average. For example, in Germany, health care costs of all mental and behavioural disorders are estimated at 10% of all health spending, with the main costs related to depression, schizophrenia and associated disorders, and anxiety disorders (Garcia-Armesto *et al.*, 2008).

However, most of the costs associated with mental health problems do not occur within the health sector, since they take the form of reduced productivity at work, absenteeism, sick leave, early retirement and receipt of disability pensions (Fajutrao *et al.*, 2009; Johnston *et al.*, 2009; Serretti *et al.*, 2009). A recent European Commission report estimated that mental health problems account for 25% of all inflow to disability benefits across the European Union. In France, 25% of illness-related social security expenditure results from stress. Substantial indirect costs are also associated with needing to provide support for mentally ill persons and their dependents. These negative economic consequences far outweigh the direct costs of treatment, and typically account for between 60% and 80% of the total economic impact of mental health problems (Valladares *et al.*, 2009).

Mental health problems are also gradually becoming, or have become, the leading cause for disability benefit claims. On average, one third of all new disability benefit claims are due to mental health conditions as the primary cause, rising to as high as 40% in some countries and almost 50% in Denmark. The share of new recipients with mental health problems is highest among young people, with around 70% of all claims in the 20-34 age groups. Mental health problems are often more often present in inflows to disability among woman than men (OECD, 2010b).

Mental health care services

Across OECD countries, mental health care services are provided in a number of settings, including within the community, through primary health care, in general and psychiatric hospitals, and in specialised mental health institutions. In recent decades, policy makers and service planners in most OECD countries have changed their approach to mental health services, moving away from large psychiatric hospitals and long-stay institutions, and increasing the reliance on home and community care.

Nevertheless, considerable and wide international variations in the structures and processes of mental health care still exist. These can be illustrated by differences in hospital statistics (*e.g.* number and type of beds, discharge rates, and lengths of stay), care settings (specialist hospitals, primary care, community care), numbers and skill mix of care providers and workforce (psychiatrists, psychologists, GPs, therapists, social workers, specialist nurses, informal carers), and rates and types of medication (*e.g.* defined daily doses of antidepressants, anxiolytics, hypnotics and sedatives) (Hermann *et al.*, 2006).

Mental health outcomes are determined in part by the availability and quality of care, and most OECD countries aim to have adequate provision for all. Assessing the sufficiency and quality of mental health care services has become one of the most difficult tasks in providing a basis for evidence-based policy across OECD countries (Hermann *et al.*, 2006). In most of the member countries the transfer from institutional to community-based mental health and addiction services has brought to light the gaps and problems with health information for that sector. It has added a degree of complexity to service delivery and evaluation of services, and it has underscored the need for reliable and current health and health care information.

Conceptual challenges

The development of reliable mental health care information systems is extremely difficult, as there are several specific hurdles for the development of mental health care information systems as compared to other areas of health care. Most of these challenges seem to be inherent to the nature of the institutional arrangements, the clinical practice and the diseases themselves. For example, the US Institute of Medicine (IOM, 2009) has issued guidelines for improvement of quality of mental health care at the system level, highlighting the complexities of measuring the performance of mental health care services (Garcia-Armesto *et al*, 2008). Distinctive characteristics of mental health care related to differences and peculiarities in diagnostic methods, treatments, the unique patient role in treatment, mode of clinician practice, and privacy and confidentiality issues all make measuring the quality of mental health care particularly challenging.

The OECD HCQI Project began work to develop indicators in the field of mental health in 2004, commencing with a survey of the availability of mental health information in OECD countries. In addition, through the use of a structured review process, expert panels have previously evaluated and recommended indicators related to four domains of quality of mental health care: treatment, continuity of care, co-ordination of care, and patient outcomes (Table 2.3). However, no explicit attempt was made to agree on definitions and boundaries for mental health.

**Table 2.3. Set of indicators recommended in OECD Health Technical Paper No. 17 (2004)
and their reported 2005 availability**

Area	Indicator name	Currently available (n countries)	Potentially available (n countries)	Total availability across countries
Continuity of care	Timely ambulatory follow-up after mental health hospitalisation	0	4	4
	Continuity of visits after hospitalisation for dual psychiatric/substance related conditions	0	2	2
	Racial/ethnic disparities in mental health follow-up rates	0	2	2
	Continuity of visits after mental health-related hospitalisation	0	4	4
Co-ordination of care	Case management for severe psychiatric disorders	1	1	2
	Visits during acute phase treatment of depression	1	1	2
Treatment	Hospital readmissions for psychiatric patients	1	8	9
	Length of treatment for substance-related disorders	1	3	4
	Use of anti-cholinergic anti-depressant drugs among elderly patients	0	8	8
	Continuous anti-depressant medication treatment in acute phase	0	2	2
	Continuous anti-depressant medication treatment in continuation phase	0	2	2
Patient outcomes	Mortality for persons with severe psychiatric conditions	3	6	9

However, the survey in 2004 revealed that systems of care vary markedly across countries, and that the availability of national indicator data suitable for international comparison was extremely limited (Garcia-Armesto *et al.*, 2008). Therefore, the following quality of care indicators were considered suitable for international comparison:

- unplanned schizophrenia re-admission rate,

- unplanned bipolar disorder re-admission rate.

Schizophrenia and bipolar disorder are among the top ten causes of years lost due to disability at the global level (WHO, 2001). Individuals with schizophrenia and other severe mental illnesses have higher mortality rates than the general population. Mortality rates tend to be significantly higher for all major causes of death but especially for suicide, with rates many times that of the general population. Such findings underline the need to provide better treatment programmes and access to care for persons with severe mental disorders, and the need to measure the quality of care they receive.

Hospital re-admission rates are widely used to measure either relapse, or complications following an inpatient stay for psychiatric and substance-use disorders. High re-admission rates for these two conditions are undesirable and point to premature discharge or lack of co-ordination with outpatient care. Given the high cost of institutional care, reducing re-admission rates can have a substantial effect on mental health spending. A recent study by the Canadian Institute for Health Information found that 20% of persons admitted to hospital for schizophrenia in Canada were re-admitted within 90 days of discharge (Garcia-Armesto *et al.*, 2008).

Longer lengths of stay, appropriate discharge planning, and follow-up visits after discharge contribute to fewer re-admissions, indicating that re-admission rates reflect the overall functioning of mental health services rather than the quality of hospital care (Lien, 2002). Thirty-day hospital re-admission rates are part of mental health performance monitoring systems in many countries, such as the Care Quality Commission in the United Kingdom, National Mental Health Performance Monitoring System and Veterans Affairs in the United States (Kilbourne *et al.*, 2010).

Findings and policy relevance

Figure 2.5 shows the variation in unplanned re-admission rates for schizophrenia, with Nordic countries at the higher end and the Slovak Republic, United Kingdom, Spain and Italy lower.

Figure 2.5. Unplanned schizophrenia re-admissions to the same hospital, 2007

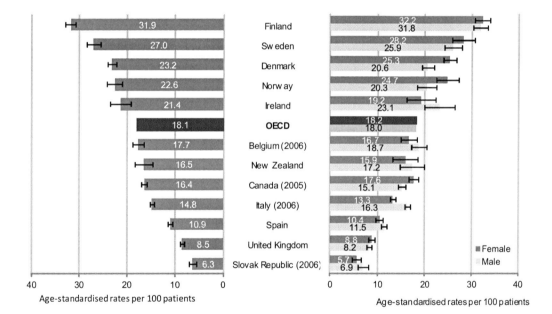

Note: Rates age-sex standardised to 2005 OECD population. 95% confidence intervals represented by H.

Source: OECD Health Care Quality Indicators Database, 2009.

The pattern of re-admission rates for bipolar disorders (Figure 2.6) is similar, with the Nordic countries well above average. Most countries have similar rates for men and women, however, male patients with schizophrenia have higher rates in Italy while female patients are more likely to be re-admitted in Canada and Denmark. Regarding bipolar disorder patients, women have higher re-admission rates in Finland, Sweden, Ireland, Canada and Belgium. These numbers may reflect differences in care-seeking behaviours or management related to a patient's gender.

Figure 2.6. Unplanned bipolar disorder re-admissions to the same hospital, 2007

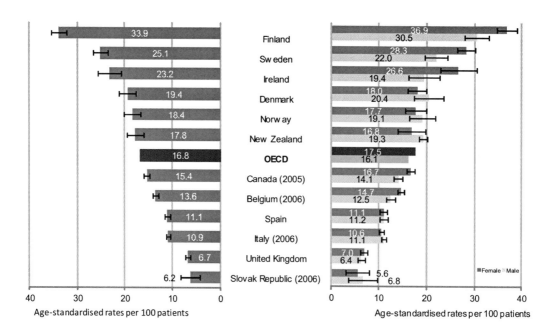

Note: Rates age-sex standardised to 2005 OECD population. 95% confidence intervals represented by H.

Source: OECD Health Care Quality Indicators Database, 2009.

Supply factors such as the availability of hospitals beds (psychiatric and total), and the profile of in-patient facilities (percentage of in-patient care provided in psychiatric hospitals, general acute hospitals or residential facilities) cannot explain the variation in re-admission rates. The average length of stay for patients with schizophrenia or bipolar disorder does not seem to be associated with variations in re-admission rates. Anecdotal evidence suggests that different approaches to crisis management might play a part. For example, some countries with lower re-admission rates, such as the United Kingdom, Spain and Italy, use community-based "crisis teams" to stabilise patients on an outpatient basis. Other countries with high rates, such as Finland and Denmark, use interval care protocols to place unstable patients into hospital care for short periods. While there is broad consensus that community-based care is preferable to in-hospital care where possible, in certain countries the practice seems to be shifting towards supplementing or substituting community-based devices with in-hospital care.

Comparability of data – the importance of unique patient identifiers

In the absence of a comparable measure of outcomes across countries, the benefits of this alternative approach are difficult to assess. The enhancement of mental health related information systems will be necessary to make this type of comparative information readily available. It is extremely important to note that the absence of unique patient identifiers in many countries does not allow the tracking of patients across facilities. Rates are therefore biased downwards as re-admissions to a different facility cannot be observed. However, the eight countries which were able to estimate re-admission rates to the same or other hospitals, show that rates based on the two different specifications were closely correlated and ranking of countries was similar, suggesting that re-admissions to the same hospital can be used as a valid approximation.

Developing better measures of mental health care quality

The limited data availability, combined with some scepticism about the long-term utility and feasibility of currently recommended indicators, led to a consensus among the OECD countries participating in the HCQI work that further developmental work would be necessary to establish a quality measurement system for mental health care. The lack of a common definition for what constitutes the mental health care system across the participating countries is a relevant issue in trying to go about measuring quality of care. Not only do terms and concepts differ, but often actual care settings and patterns of diagnoses differ widely across countries.

A second matter of concern is a lack of knowledge about the components of information systems containing data linked to mental health care, and the nature of these data across countries. Therefore, in 2008 a survey was conducted to explore the possibilities for measuring the quality of mental health care, and to identify potential indicators to be included in OECD's HCQI set, seeking to gather information on three areas of interest for the description of national information systems linked to mental health services:

- Types of mental health data available at system level;

- Data sources available at national level;

- Institutional arrangements framing ownership and use of the information system.

The main conclusions are summarised below:

- The availability of data across countries is generally very good for some types of data (structure and activity) and problematic for others. In order to measure process and outcome of mental health care, data on treatment and procedures, together with mental morbidity individual data and specific mortality data would be required. Examining the figures, there is a clear need to improve information systems across OECD countries in this respect. Nevertheless, many of the countries where this type of information is not currently available are already undertaking some kind of reform along these lines, so the availability of these data can be expected to improve significantly in the short term.

- The data sources currently most widely available across countries are hospital administrative databases, national surveys and national registries. This should be taken into account in the selection of mental health care quality indicators for the first phase of data collection.

- The expansion of the availability of the unique patient identifier would mean a real step forward in terms of ability to track patients across settings and levels of care. Strict anonymisation protocols would be required to make full use of this tool while preserving confidentiality. However, the introduction of a unique patient identifier does not seem to be evolving in parallel with the degree of development of administrative data sources at the primary care and community care levels. This can pose problems to build indicators assessing continuity of care and quality of prescription or treatment at this level. That is especially important because most of mental health care is provided out of the hospital across OECD countries.

- The integration of information systems across different levels of care provision is low. Reinforcing this feature of information systems will be of paramount importance in order to pursue data to measure continuity of care.

- The integration between mental health care information and physical health information is reasonably good at hospital level. This can allow for outcome indicators linking somatic and mental health.

- The decisions about the data items to be collected are often made centrally, aiming to support planning and management and in some cases reimbursement. Data collection is mainly bottom up through administrators and health care professionals. Therefore, the shaping of information systems to allow for quality assessment at the system level should be reasonably attainable. Common problems exist with data reporting and compliance; in most of the cases, data recording is perceived as routine activity by the personnel involved, though it is often considered an additional burden. The use of this type of information for consumers' information or public accountability is infrequent across countries.

- Coding varies from country to country, but in general it is changing in the direction of ICD-10. This general trend should be taken into account in specifying the indicators to be collected, while contemplating the translation of the relevant codes into the other classifications in use across countries.

Summary

The development of mental health care indicators and information systems is more difficult than for other areas of health care. This is mainly due to the complex nature of mental health disorders, the wide differences in diagnostic and therapeutic practices, institutional governance barriers, as well as differences in the coding and reporting of mental health care within and between countries. In addition, information systems in social, long-term and informal care settings are generally less developed than health care settings, and are not always interoperable. Confidentiality is another serious challenge: mental health conditions are more prone to raise privacy and data protection issues than most other areas of care. The expansion of the availability of the unique patient identifier, standardisation of coding practices, and integration of information systems across different levels of care would mean a real step forward in terms of ability to track patients across settings and levels of care.

2.5.   Cancer care

Importance and relevance

Cancer is one of the major public health issues in OECD countries. It is either the first or second cause of death (after cardiovascular disease), accounting for more than a quarter of all deaths in many countries, while at least one-third of cancer can be prevented, and a further third can be either detected early or effectively treated. The WHO estimates that worldwide, in 2004, it accounted for 7.4 million deaths (or 13% of all deaths). This figure is projected to continue to rise to an estimated 12 million deaths in 2030.

The incidence, morbidity, and mortality burden of different types of cancer differ within and between regions, across demographic and social profiles of (sub) populations, and across individual co-morbidity profiles. This makes measurement of the quality of cancer care an especially challenging area. In addition there are the different elements of care involved in the natural history of cancers – prevention, early detection and screening, diagnostic evaluation, primary and adjuvant therapy, post-treatment surveillance and follow-up care, treatment of recurrent cancers, palliative care and end of life care. A further complicating factor is that these pathways are not necessarily sequential as several of the elements may occur simultaneously.

In response to the burden of cancer disease and in recognition of the potential to achieve improved health gains, cancer control strategies have been introduced in many OECD countries. Most national cancer control programmes include every aspect of care, from prevention and early detection to curative treatment and palliative care. These programmes are typically supported by the robust scientific evidence. The strength of these programmes lies in their comprehensive approach in identifying priority cancers and in identifying areas where specific developments have a greater likelihood of impacting on morbidity and mortality. Developments in new technologies, diagnosis and treatment constantly shift and hence cancer control programmes have to be sufficiently flexible to be update periodically. The more recent national cancer control programmes include the development of frameworks to foster a co-ordinated and consistent approach to the delivery of cancer care.

Internationally, there are several collaborative initiatives measuring, analysing and reporting cancer data using population-based cancer registries. The WHO's International Association of Cancer Registries (IACR) publishes *Cancer Incidence in Five Continents* and GLOBOCAN, synthesised under CANCERMondial, the world's largest databases of information on the global burden of cancer incidence. The NORDCAN Project presents the incidence, mortality and prevalence of 41 major cancers in the Nordic countries. The EUROCARE Project (European cancer registry-based study on the survival and care of cancer patients) uses data from 93 population-based cancer registries in 23 European countries to measure, analyse and report survival rates of cancer patients in Europe, and to detect variations between regions over time. EUROCHIP is another research network focused on developing the European cancer health indicators set and a series of specific actions to address cancer inequalities. The CONCORD Study researches cancer survival worldwide, quantifying international differences in population-based relative survival by age, sex, country and region for breast, colon, rectum and prostate cancers. The WHO International Agency for Research on Cancer (IARC) has recently launched the European Cancer Observatory. The work developed by IARC extends beyond Europe reaching a worldwide scope and produces regular reports on the epidemiology of cancer around the world, their most recent report was published in 2008.

Box 2.2. Policies on quality of cancer care in England

On 6th July 2010, the Secretary of State for Health, Andrew Lansley, and the Minister for Care Services, Paul Burstow, asked Professor Sir Mike Richards, the National Cancer Director, to review the Cancer Reform Strategy (CRS) to ensure that England has the right strategy, to deliver improved survival rates. In addition to focusing on outcomes, the review will set the future direction for cancer services.

The CRS was launched on 3 December 2007 and set out a wide range of actions to build on the significant progress made on cancer since the publication of the Calman-Hine report in 1995 and the NHS Cancer Plan in 2000. The strategy includes measures intended to improve cancer prevention and speed up the diagnosis and treatment of cancer.

One initiative that came out of the CRS was the National Awareness and Early Diagnosis Initiative (NAEDI), which has been working since 2008 to improve the public's awareness of the signs and symptoms of cancer and encouraging those with symptoms to seek help earlier than they currently do. It also aims to support primary health care professionals to diagnose cancer earlier. It has been calculated that bringing survival rates into line with the best of those in Europe could save up to 10 000 lives a year. The review of the CRS will be looking at how best to achieve this.

NHS Cancer Screening Programmes play a key role in the early identification of cancers. The NHS Breast Screening Programme in England began in 1988 and is internationally regarded for its coverage and quality. Experts estimate the programme saves 1 400 lives per year. The CRS committed to extending the programme to women aged 47-73 and all local breast screening units are expected to begin the extension in 2010-11. The NHS Bowel Screening Programme began rolling-out in 2006 and is one of the first national bowel screening programmes in the world. Around 2 million men and women are screened each year, detecting around 3000 cases of bowel cancer. The programme is expected to reduce mortality from bowel cancer by 16%, and is currently being extended to men and women aged 70 to 75. The NHS Cervical Screening Programme began in 1988 and screens women from the age of 25. Experts estimate it saves up to 4 500 lives every year. The NHS Operating Framework for 2010-11 has stated that all women should receive the results of their cervical screening tests within two weeks by the end of 2010.

The CRS also extended the scope of the cancer waiting times standards set out in the NHS Cancer Plan 2000. The current standards are:

- All patients with suspected cancer who are urgently referred by their GP should be seen by a specialist within two weeks;

- All patients with cancer should wait no longer than 31 days from diagnosis to first treatment; and

- There should be no longer than 62 days from an urgent GP referral to their first treatment.

The OECD's HCQI Project has focused on breast, cervical and colorectal cancers – these were selected on the basis of the scale of their burden and also because there are important public health interventions for each of these cancers. The indicators variants that were used are as follows:

- Cancer five-year survival rates (breast, cervical and colorectal cancers);

- Cancer mortality rates (all, breast, cervical, colon, lung and prostate cancers);

- Screening rates (breast and cervical cancers).

Conceptual challenges

Three cancer care indicators are collected by the OECD, offering one measure related to early detection of cancer (screening rates), and two complementary measures allowing for cross-country comparisons of cancer care outcome (survival and mortality).

Screening rates

Screening rates for cancer reflect the proportion of patients who are eligible for a screening test that actually receive the test. Because policies regarding screening periodicity and target age group differ across countries, the rates are based on each country's specific policy.

Survival rates

Survival rate is highly sensitive to policy changes and thus extremely useful in monitoring the impact of new interventions or innovations in diagnosis or treatment. However, survival is also a complex notion to interpret: longer survival may reflect earlier diagnosis, over-diagnosis or later death; the so called lead time bias due to improved screening implies earlier detection resulting in a longer observation period and, thus, longer survival. This does not necessarily translate into a later death.

Relative cancer survival rates reflect the proportion of patients with a certain type of cancer who are still alive after a specified time period (commonly five years) compared to the survival prospects of a comparator group who do not have cancer. Relative survival rates capture the excess mortality that can be attributed to the diagnosis. To illustrate, a relative survival rate of 80% does not mean that 80% of the cancer patients are still alive after five years, but that 80% of the patients that were expected to be alive after five years, given their gender and age at diagnosis, are in fact still alive.

Mortality rates

Mortality rates are numbers of deaths registered in a country divided by the size of the corresponding population. The cancer mortality data reflect the differences in medical training and practice as well as in death certification procedures across countries (for further detail on the specific nature of these differences see (Mathers *et al.*, 2005).

Mortality rates alone are not sufficient to draw inferences about quality of care. This is because mortality reflects the effect of a whole range of inputs to cancer care – primary prevention, stage at which diagnosis took place, effectiveness and timeliness of acute treatment, rehabilitation etc. Thus, both survival and mortality measures should be considered in interpreting trends and exploring cross-country differences in cancer care.

Findings and policy relevance

Screening, survival and mortality for cervical cancer

While cervical cancer is no longer among the most common forms of cancer or cancer-related deaths, it is of great interest to policy makers because it is largely preventable. Screening by regular pelvic exam and pap smears can identify premalignant lesions, which can be effectively treated. Regular screening also increases the probability of early detection of malignancy which in turn can have a dramatic impact on survival prospects (Gatta *et al.*, 1998). Consequently, OECD countries have instituted screening programmes with specific periodicity and target groups. In addition, promising cancer preventing vaccines have been developed, based on the discovery that cervical cancer is caused by sexual transmission of certain forms of the human papillomavirus (Harper *et al.*, 2006).

Screening rates vary widely across countries with Austria, Norway, the United Kingdom and Sweden achieving coverage of around 80% of the target population

(Figure 2.7). Some countries with very low screening rates, like Turkey and the Slovak Republic, do not yet have uniform national screening programmes (as of 2008). In these instances, low rates reflect local programmes or opportunistic screening. The data indicates that screening rates in several countries slightly declined between 2000 and 2008.

Figure 2.7. Cervical cancer screening, percentage of women screened age 20-69, 2000 to 2008 (or nearest available year)

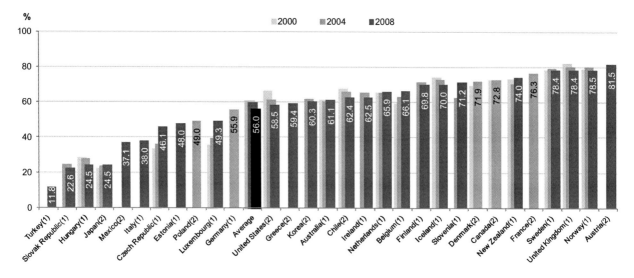

1. Programme.
2. Survey.

Source: OECD Health Data 2010.

Relative survival rates are commonly used to track progress in treating a disease over time as they reflect both how early the cancer was detected and the effectiveness of the treatment provided. Nearly all countries recorded five-year relative survival rates above 60% for the period 2002-07. The rates ranged from 76.5% in Korea to 50.1% in Poland (Figure 2.8). Over the periods 1997-2002 and 2002-07, the five-year relative rates improved in most countries, although in most instances the increase is not statistically significant.

Coinciding with the decreasing trend in incidence, between 1998 and 2008 the mortality rates for cervical cancer declined for most OECD countries, with larger improvements for Mexico, Iceland and Denmark (Figure 2.9). Nevertheless, the rates are still high in Mexico and eastern European countries.

Figure 2.8. Cervical cancer five-year relative survival rate, 1997-2002 and 2002-07 (or nearest available period)

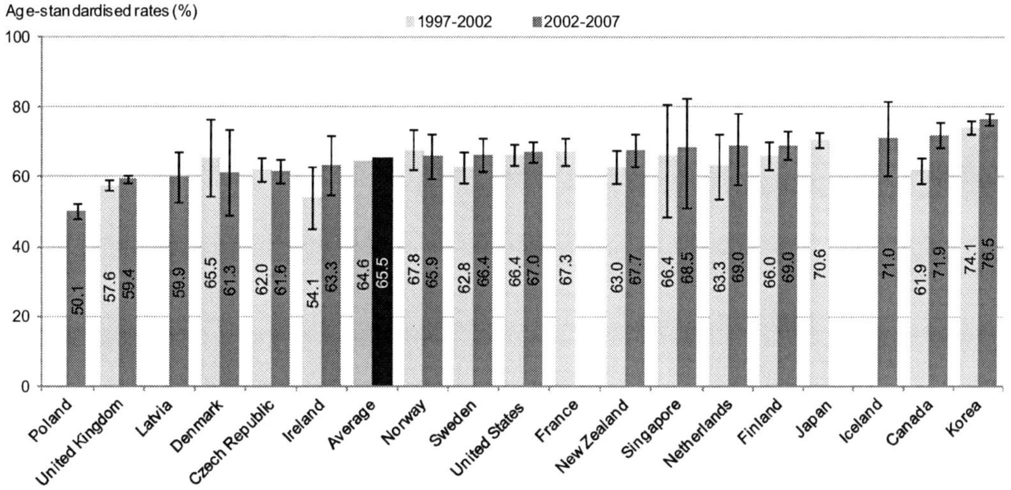

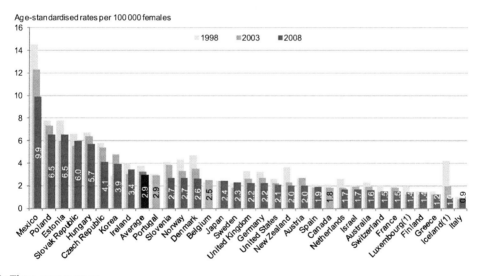

Note: Rates age-standardised to International Cancer Survival Standards population. 95% confidence intervals represented by H.

Source: OECD Health Care Quality Indicators Database, 2009.

Figure 2.9. Cervical cancer mortality, females, 1998 to 2008 (or nearest available year)

1: Three-year average

Source: OECD Health Data 2010 (extracted from WHO Mortality Database and age-standardised to 1980 OECD population).

Screening, survival and mortality for breast cancer

Breast cancer is the most common form of cancer in women, accounting for 27% of cancer incidence and 16% of cancer mortality for most OECD countries (Ferlay *et al.*, 2010). Overall spending for breast cancer care typically amounts to about 0.5-0.6% of total health care expenditure (OECD, 2003).

Most countries have adopted breast cancer screening programmes, although the optimal frequency of screening and the target age-group are still the subject of debate. For European countries, EU guidelines (2006) promote a target screening rate of at least 75% of eligible women. In Finland and the Netherlands, almost 85% of women aged 50-69 years are screened whereas in Turkey, Poland, the Slovak Republic, and Denmark rates are below 20% (Figure 2.10). In some countries with very low screening rates, like Turkey, Denmark and Poland, national screening programmes have not yet been rolled out (as of 2008), and as is the case for cervical cancer screening, the low rates reflect opportunistic screening or local programmes. Some countries which had low rates in the early 2000s, such as the Czech Republic, Korea and France, showed substantial increases by 2008, whereas some countries with already high rates experienced declines, including Norway, Finland and the United Kingdom.

Figure 2.10. Mammography screening, percentage of women aged 50-69 screened, 2000 to 2008 (or nearest available year)

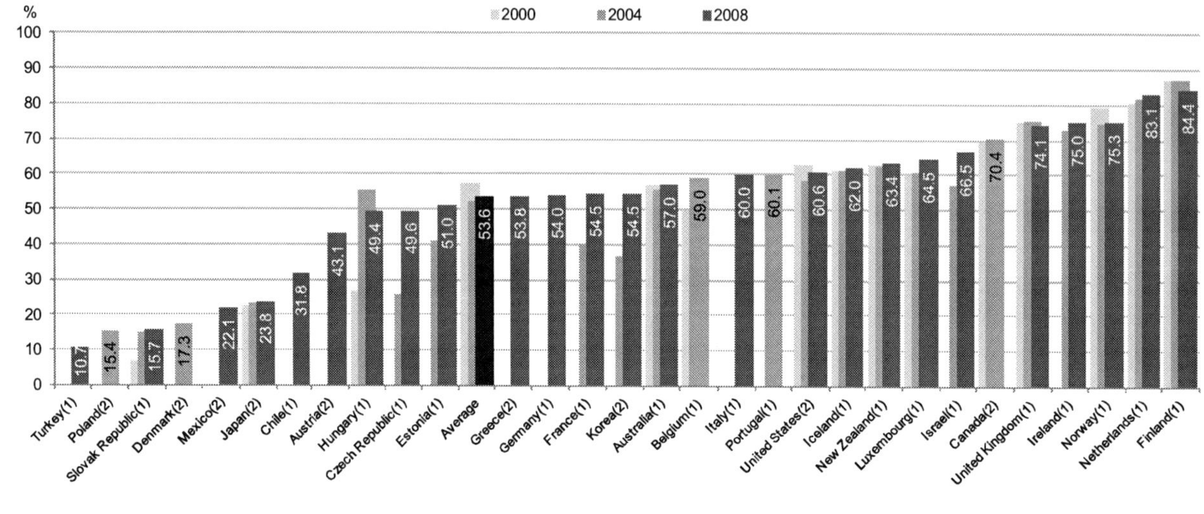

1. Programme.

2. Survey.

Source: OECD Health Data 2010

The combination of public health interventions and improved medical technology has contributed to substantial improvements in survival rates for breast cancer. Greater awareness of the disease and the promotion of self-examination and screening mammography has also led to improvements in detecting the disease at earlier stages – a factor that has a significant bearing on survival prospects. In addition, clinical studies have demonstrated that technological improvements in the treatment of breast cancer have increased survival as well as the quality of life of survivors (Mauri *et al.*, 2008).

Across countries, although the overall trend in breast cancer survival rates shows an improvement between 1997-2002 and 2002-07, the changes are typically not statistically significant (Figure 2.11). Data over a longer time period confirm that five-year survival rates for breast cancer have increased over recent years particularly in eastern European countries that historically had lower survival rates (Verdecchia *et al.*, 2007).

**Figure 2.11. Breast cancer five-year relative survival rate, 1997-2002 and 2002-07
(or nearest available period)**

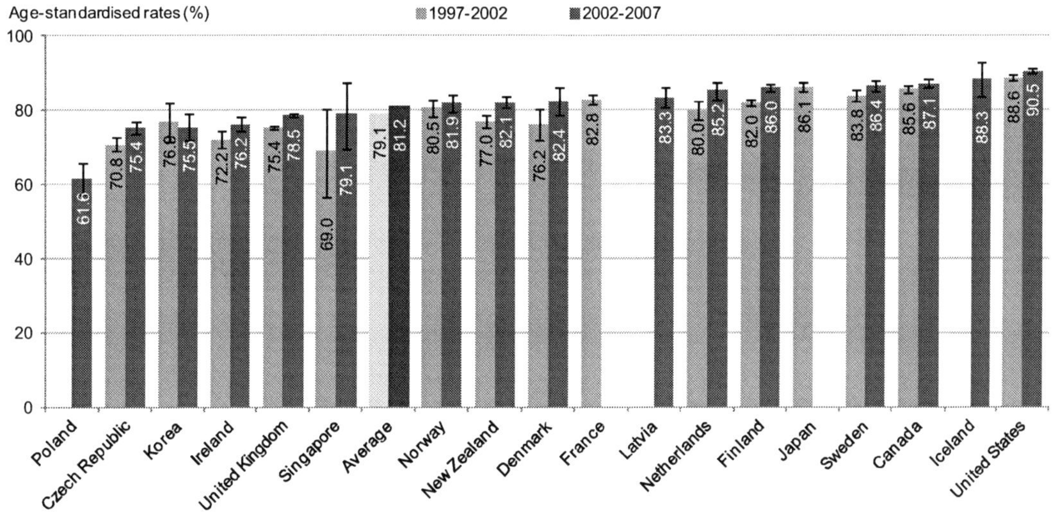

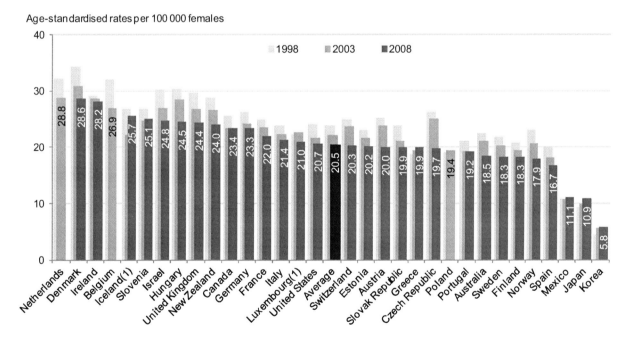

Note: Rates are age-standardised to the International Cancer Survival Standards population and 95% confidence intervals are represented by H.).

Source: OECD Health Care Quality Indicators Data 2009.

Figure 2.12. Breast cancer mortality, females, 1998 to 2008 (or nearest available year)

1. Rates for Iceland and Luxembourg are based on a three-year average.

Source: OECD Health Data 2010 (extracted from the WHO Mortality Database and age-standardised to the 1980 OECD population).

Many countries have survival rates of over 80%, with rates as high as 90% for the United States (Figure 2.11). Given that the impact of improved rates of early detection are not immediately apparent, the impact of the decrease in mammography rates between 2000 and 2006 in Norway and Finland will remain uncertain until survival data for future years become available.

While there has been an increase in incidence rates of breast cancer in many OECD countries, mortality rates have declined or remained stable over the past decade (Figure 2.12). This trend probably reflects increased survival due to earlier diagnosis and/or better treatments. Korea and Japan are the exceptions, though the changes are small and mortality levels continue to be the lowest among OECD countries. Conversely, improvements are substantial for countries that had higher levels in the 1990s such as the Czech Republic, Hungary and Denmark but other countries including Norway also experienced a larger improvement.

Survival and mortality for colorectal cancer

Colorectal cancer is the third most common form of cancer in both women (after breast and lung cancers) and men (after prostate and lung cancers). It is estimated that approximately USD 8.4 billion is spent in the United States each year on the treatment of colorectal cancer (Brown *et al.*, 2002).

Advances in diagnosis and treatment have increased survival over the last decades. Better screening with tests for occult blood or routine colonoscopy, have increased the number of cases that are diagnosed at a pre-cancerous or early stage (Midgley and Kerr, 1999). There is still an active debate in many countries about the best approach to screening (Davila, 2006). While colonoscopy is widely considered the most effective approach, as it allows full inspection of the colon and the instantaneous removal of potentially pre-cancerous polyps, many countries are concerned about the cost implications of and the capacity required for population-based colonoscopy, and data on screening rates for colorectal cancer are not yet available at an international level.

Existing evidence illustrates the clinical benefit of screening with routine colonoscopy and stool tests for occult blood (USPSTF, 2009). Good evidence also exists in support of various treatment modalities, such as surgery (Govindarajan *et al.*, 2006) and chemotherapy (CCCG, 2000), even for advanced stages of the disease. The same literature, however, suggests that screening and treatment options are not sufficiently utilised. Variation in outcomes for patients with colorectal cancer is captured by five-year relative survival rates and mortality rates.

Japan has the highest relative survival rate of 67%, followed by Iceland and the United States with rates above 65% (Figure 2.13). Poland has the lowest rate with 38%, followed by Latvia and the Czech Republic.

Figure 2.13. Colorectal cancer, five-year relative survival rate, total and male/female (latest period)

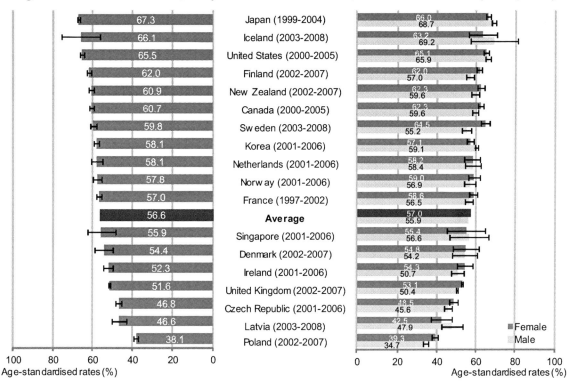

Note: Rates age-standardised to International Cancer Survival Standards population. 95% confidence intervals represented by H.

Source: OECD Health Care Quality Indicators Database, 2009.

Figure 2.14. Colorectal cancer, five-year relative survival rate, 1997-2002 and 2002-07 (or nearest available period)

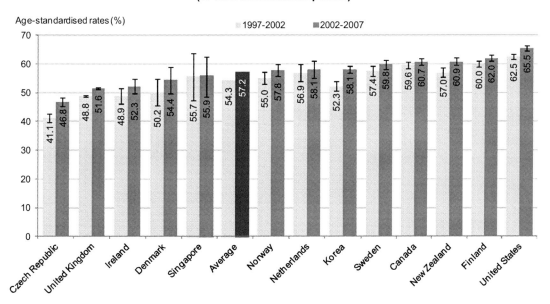

Note: Rates age-standardised to International Cancer Survival Standards population. 95% confidence intervals represented by H.

Source: OECD Health Care Quality Indicators Database, 2009.

All countries show improvement in survival rates over time (Figure 2.14), although the increase is often not statistically significant. The United States, which had the highest survival rate of 62.5% for patients diagnosed in 1997-2002 improved to 65.5% for those diagnosed in 2000-05. The Czech Republic improved from 41% to 47% between 1997-2002 and 2001-06.

Historical data from France shows that the five-year survival rate between 1976 and 1988 increased from 33% to 55%. This is attributed to higher resection rates with lower post-operative mortality, earlier diagnosis and increased use of chemotherapy (Faivre-Finn *et al.*, 2002). These findings are consistent with results from other European countries (Sant *et al.*, 2009) and the United States (SEER, 2009). Recent data from the EUROCARE Project showed that survival for colorectal cancer continued to increase in Europe, and in particular in eastern European countries (Verdecchia *et al.*, 2007).

Most countries experienced a decrease in mortality for colorectal cancer between 1998 and 2008 (Figure 2.15). While Korea's rates have increased markedly over time, these rates are still among the lowest in OECD countries. The rapid introduction of western-type diet is a possible explanation for this increase. Korea has achieved a significant increase in relative survival rates over recent years, indicating that the health care system is addressing this new challenge. Central and eastern European countries tend to have higher mortality rates with no clear geographic pattern emerging for the other OECD countries. Countries with high relative survival rates, like Japan, Iceland and the United States also have below-average mortality rates, which supports the hypothesis that the differences in relative survival reflect better cancer care.

Figure 2.15. Colorectal cancer mortality, 1998 to 2008 (or nearest available year)

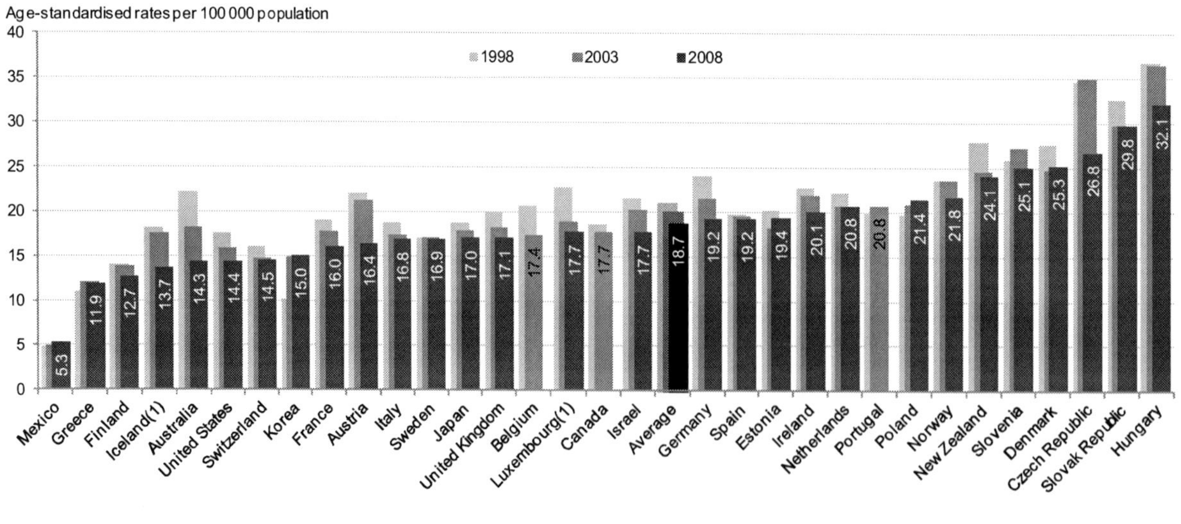

Source: OECD Health Data 2010 (extracted from WHO Mortality Database and age-standardised to 1980 OECD population).

Operational and methodological challenges

Significant progress has been made within the HCQI Project and by individual member countries in improving data comparability for the cancer indicators. Much effort has been made to implement data quality standards and confidence intervals, to resolve differences in definitions and to introduce standard procedures for age and sex adjustment. For example, on a range of survey indicators (such as cancer screening), countries have been able to alter national reporting standards (for instance in reporting age group) to provide the OECD with comparable data.

Several methodological issues persist relating to cancer data collection and indicator calculation. These include, the extent to which country data are truly nationally representative, data sourcing (*e.g.* surveys *vs.* registries), heterogeneity in cancer survival and screening reporting periods, age standardisation and significantly, a lack of cancer staging data.

Non-nationally representative cancer survival rates

Some countries are unable to provide nationally representative data for cancer survival. This is particularly the case for countries whose cancer registries do not cover their entire territory. Presenting nationally and non-nationally representative data together can confuse and invalidate cross-national comparisons.

Data sources – presentation of administrative versus survey data for cancer screening

Data for breast and cervical cancer screening can come from varying sources across countries, namely administrative and programmatic data or household surveys. Registries for prevention activities often do not cover opportunistic screening and settings outside the health care system like community centres, local campaigns, and charities. Data from these sources therefore underestimate the actual screening rate. Survey sources have the drawback of recall bias and sensitivity to the survey methodology. Estimating the overall impact of these issues and their effects on cross country comparisons is very difficult.

Heterogeneity in cancer survival and screening reporting periods

An additional issue with the cancer screening and cancer survival data is that reporting periods differ widely across countries. In the area of cancer survival, countries also have widely varying time periods from which they are presenting data, since many countries do not compile their cancer survival statistics annually, but rather every three or five years, depending on the periodicity of the data system.

Age adjustment – updating and truncating the standard population

Age standardisation is necessary since a country's age structure, depending on the nature of the disease and the structure of the population, can influence the international comparison of health system performance. To account for such differences in age structure, age adjustments are made based on standardised populations.

Survival rates have been age-standardised using the International Cancer Survival Standard (ICSS) population. It appears that the use of a truncated version of the OECD standard population (at age 45+, thus shaping the age structure more closely to cancer disease specific populations) may provide better estimates, although the differences may be more important for some types of cancers (*e.g.* cervical cancer) than for others.

Staging data

Routine data from cancer registries often lack information on stage of cancer at diagnosis, thereby limiting their use. Such staging information is extremely important at both individual and population levels. Staging data are crucial for diagnosis, prognosis and treatment and therefore have a significant impact on effective clinical decision making. Furthermore, without staging information it is not possible to assess whether increases in measured survival are due to earlier detection or better treatment outcomes. More information about staging will enable the proper measurement and evaluation of the actual quality of cancer care.

Next steps

The OECD HCQI Project has expanded work on the quality of cancer care performance. Cancer care has been identified as a top priority due to the maturity of available indicators and the policy relevance of cancer mortality across OECD countries. The first phase involved the development of a conceptual framework model and macrolevel analysis based on readily available HCQI and *OECD Health Data*. The work illustrated the importance of having cancer control strategies and highlighted the need to investigate the institutional characteristics of cancer care systems across countries.

Analysis of differences in survival rates indicates that most of differences in cancer survival could be explained by countries' income, available resources and investment in cancer care in terms of technology and innovative drugs. The characteristics of the system such as timely access to service (including screening and waiting time from diagnosis to initial treatment) and the effective execution of cancer care in terms of combined surgery/chemotherapy/radiotherapy, case management and multidisciplinary team approach are also highly correlated with cancer survival. The remaining differences may be explained by cancer policy characteristics such as setting specific objectives and timeframes, ensuring proper monitoring and quality assurance and making someone responsible for meeting the targets.

This ongoing analytical work will proceed in collaboration with key organisations and projects with international expertise in this area, including the CONCORD Study which has recently undertaken an international comparison of survival rates and the EUROCARE study which follows the survival of cancer patients in Europe.

2.6.   Patient safety

Importance and relevance

Patient safety has recently become one of the most prominent issues in health policy. A growing body of evidence indicating high rates of medical errors and their disastrous consequences to patients and their families is now rightfully challenging the trust that patients and policy makers have bestowed on the medical profession. These potentially preventable events can also result in unnecessary re-admissions and longer hospital stays leading to significant waste of scarce health care resources and economic costs for patients.

While it is difficult to measure system wide costs, it is estimated that the United States spends between USD 17-24 billion per year on preventable adverse events (Kohn and Donaldson, 2000), with cost estimates for hospitals ranging from USD 4 000 to USD 40 000 per preventable event (Loveland *et al.*, 2008). As early as 1991, the landmark Harvard Medical Practice Study found that significant adverse events, such as wrong-site surgery or medication errors, occur in nearly 4% of all hospital admissions (Brennan *et al.*, 2004). However, such results did not receive widespread attention until the US Institute of Medicine integrated the available evidence on medical errors and estimated that more people die from medical errors than from traffic injuries or breast cancer (Kohn and Donaldson, 2000). More recently, these findings have been confirmed and extended by health services researchers from around the world. Some studies have shown that the adverse events rate is more that 10% among patients admitted to hospital (Ackroyd-Stolarz *et al.*, 2009). The safety of hospitalised patients is now recognised as a global problem (de Vries *et al.*, 2008; Brady *et al.*, 2009) that requires urgent attention in every OECD country.

Box 2.3. The recommendation on patient safety by the European Commission

An estimated 8-12% of patients admitted to hospital in the European Union suffer from adverse events whilst receiving health care. Adverse events include: health care-associated infections (accounting for approximately 25% of adverse events), medication-related errors, surgical errors, medical device failures, errors in diagnosis or failure to act on the results of tests. Much of the harm to patients is preventable, but the implementation of strategies to reduce harm varies widely across the European Union.

To help prevent and reduce the occurrence of adverse events in health care in June 2009, the Council of the European Union adopted the Recommendation on Patient Safety, including the prevention and control of health care-associated infections. Actions recommended in the document include:

- Standardisation of patient safety measures, definitions and terminology. The member states are at different levels of development and implementation of patient safety strategies. It is recommended that common terminology, as well as patient safety standards and best practices be developed and shared amongst member states.

- Greater reporting of patient safety events. It is recommended that more comprehensive reporting on adverse events take place, in a blame-free manner. This will help monitor and control patient safety, but also provide data on the effectiveness of implemented measures.

- Education and training of health care workers, focusing on patient safety. Patient safety should be embedded in the education and training of all health workers, including on-the-job training and the development of core competencies in patient safety.

- Greater awareness of patient safety amongst patients. Patients themselves need to be aware of the authorities responsible for patient safety, the patient safety measures and standards which are in place, and available complaints procedures.

A report on progress with implementation of the Recommendation is due by the European Commission in June 2012. As next step, the Commission is reflecting with member states on possible EU action on wider quality of health care. Four objectives of such action have been identified:

- To achieve a common understanding of health care quality in EU member states.

- To promote continuous health care quality improvement in all member states.

- To improve comparability of collected data.

- To establish a culture of mutual learning among EU member states.

In order to reach the above objectives, enhanced collaboration on health care quality between EU member states is necessary. The Commission is currently looking into the possibility of organising and co-financing such collaboration.

In response, substantial effort has gone into understanding the root causes of medical errors, developing typologies to categorise them, and implementing initiatives to reduce them. The World Alliance for Patient Safety, sponsored by the World Health Organization, aims to increase awareness and political commitment to improve the safety of care, it also facilitates the development of patient safety policy and practice. An International Classification of Patient Safety has been developed to help elicit, capture and analyse factors relevant to patient safety in a manner conducive to learning and system improvement. Most national governments and the European Commission have undertaken their own initiatives to measure and improve patient safety.

Conceptual challenges: selecting and constructing indicators

Collecting information on patient safety events from OECD member countries is part of the conceptual framework of the OECD's work on health systems comparisons (Arah *et al.*, 2006) and is an important module in the OECD Health Care Quality Indicators Project. To advance this work, the OECD convened an international expert panel in 2004, which rigorously evaluated 59 candidate indicators of patient safety and endorsed 21 for international use (McLoughlin, Millar *et al.*, 2006). Twelve of these indicators came from a larger set developed and maintained by the US Agency for Healthcare Research and Quality (AHRQ), known as the AHRQ Patient Safety Indicators (PSIs). PSI definitions are in the public domain and have been harmonised for international use by a collaborative group that included experts from six OECD countries (Quan *et al.*, 2008).

At the first meeting of the HCQI Patient Safety Subgroup, hosted by the Irish Department of Health and Children in 2006, country experts agreed to advance two important initiatives: *1)* adapting hospital administrative data systems to assess patient safety internationally, and *2)* reviewing adverse event reporting systems to evaluate their usability for the same purpose. Under the first initiative, patient safety indicator data have been collected over three cycles since 2007 (Drösler *et al.*, 2009), with increasing interest over this time among OECD countries (Table 2.4). Details of the 2009 data are available in the OECD Health Working Paper No. 47.

Table 2.4. Patient safety indicator data collections under the auspices of the OECD HCQI Project

Year	2007	2008	2009
Number of participating countries	7	16	19

Based on the results of experimental pilot calculations in 2007 and 2008, seven PSIs were identified by the expert group as suitable for ongoing international data collection given the availability of data from national data systems:

- Catheter-related bloodstream infection;

- Post-operative pulmonary embolism (PE) or deep vein thrombosis (DVT);

- Postoperative sepsis;

- Accidental puncture or laceration;

- Foreign body left in during procedure;

- Obstetric trauma – vaginal delivery with instrument;

- Obstetric trauma – vaginal delivery without instrument.

The data source for these indicators is hospital administrative data. Typically these include diagnoses codes classified according to the International Classification of Diseases, procedures classified according to each country's own system, patient demographic characteristics (*e.g.* age, sex), and information on the type of admission (*e.g.* elective, emergency) and discharge status (*e.g.* discharged to home, deceased). In contrast to dedicated safety reporting systems that are designed to help uncover the root causes of adverse events in a non-punitive and confidential manner, administrative data mainly serve other purposes, such as billing or activity reporting. As such they tend to lack detailed clinical information required for root cause analyses. To reduce variation in PSI rates due to international differences in these data systems, each country extracted its PSI data according to a detailed calculation manual with specific code lists for each indicator. The four indicators described in the following paragraphs are considered fit for public reporting by the Health Care Quality Indicator expert group.

Main findings: operational and methodological challenges

Depending on the indicator, moderate to substantial variation in PSI rates across countries was found (Table 2.5).

Table 2.5. Minimum and maximum non-standardised PSI rates (%) reported by 18 countries in 2009; one country withdrew its data

Indicator (number of countries reporting data)	Min rate (%)	Max rate (%)	Ratio between highest and lowest PSI rate
Foreign body left in during procedure (n = 15)	0.002	0.011	**5.5**
Catheter-related bloodstream infection (n = 16)	0.004	0.425	**106.25**
Postoperative pulmonary embolism (PE) or deep vein thrombosis (DVT) (n = 15)	0.108	1.450	**13.50**
Postoperative sepsis (n = 16)	0.140	8.081	**57.73**
Accidental Puncture or Laceration (n=15)	0.013	0.402	**31.15**
Obstetric trauma – vaginal delivery with instrument (n = 18)	1.556	16.626	**10.69**
Obstetric trauma – vaginal delivery without instrument (n = 18)	0.193	3.811	**19.75**

Obstetric trauma

The obstetric indicators have been integrated in several national quality evaluation programmes, with countries having greater familiarity in their monitoring. Variation in country-specific rates is therefore more likely to reflect real differences rather than variations in data quality (Figures 2.16 and 2.17). For example, caesarean delivery rates are known to vary between 14% and 40% across OECD countries. Furthermore, the definitions of the obstetric indicators do not focus on secondary diagnoses but rely on the main (principal) diagnosis in most cases for which data tend to be less problematic.

Figure 2.16. Obstetric trauma after vaginal delivery with instrument, 2007

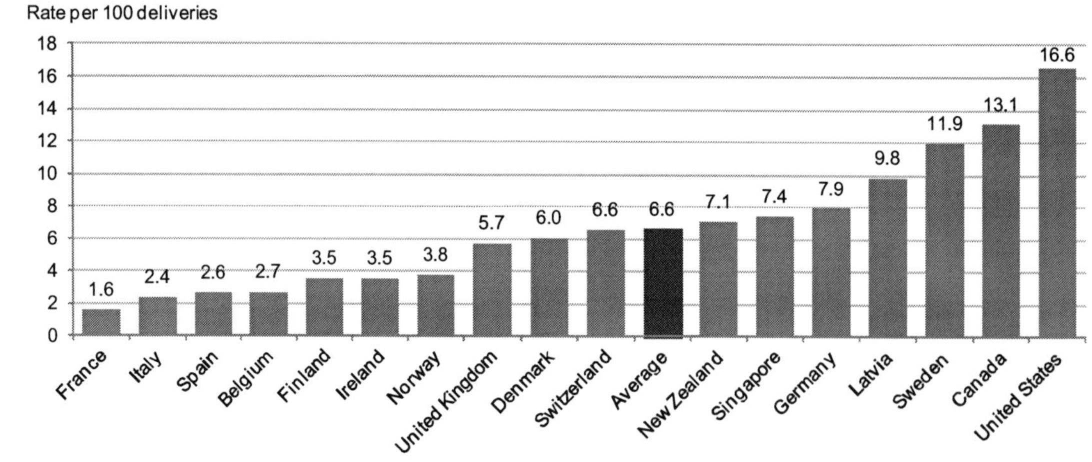

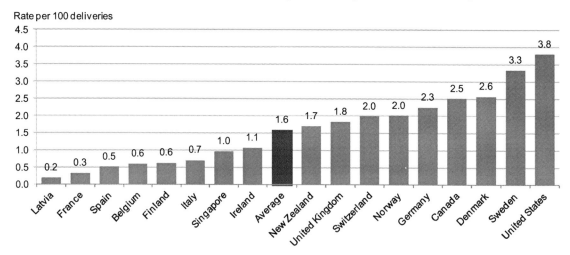

Note: Rates are not standardised. Rates for Italy, Belgium, Switzerland and the United States refer to 2006; rates for Denmark refer to 2008.

Source: OECD Health Care Quality Database 2009.

Figure 2.17. Obstetric trauma after vaginal delivery without instrument, 2007

Note: Rates are not standardised. Rates for Italy, Belgium, Switzerland and the United States refer to 2006; rates for Denmark refer to 2008.

Source: OECD Health Care Quality Database 2009.

Foreign body left in during procedure

The foreign body left in during procedure indicator shows relatively low prevalence and variation across OECD countries (Table 2.5). Rather low rates in general reflect the nature of a sentinel event indicator. While all patient safety indicators refer to events that should occur rarely, sentinel events (including foreign body left in during procedure, transfusion reaction, wrong site surgery, etc.) are those that in theory and practice should never occur. Rate should be close to zero and each positive event should stand as an alert for immediate careful analysis as this may reflect institutional quality problems (Figure 2.18).

Figure 2.18. Foreign body left in during procedure rates per 100 000 discharges, 2007

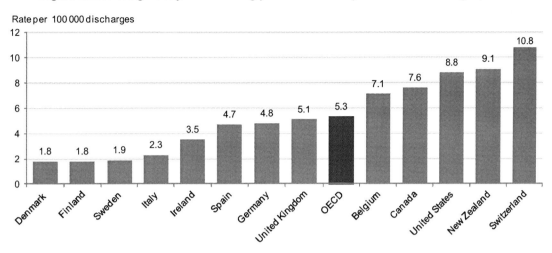

Note: Data for Denmark refer to 2008 and for Belgium and the United States, data refer to 2006. Cases with the critical incident present on hospital admission are excluded in the Canadian data.

Source: OECD Health Care Quality Database 2009.

The accidental puncture or laceration indicator rates vary across participating OECD countries between 13 and 356 events per 100 000 discharges (0.01 and 0.4%) (Figure 2.19). However, interpretation is not straight forward. Underreporting may be a concern for countries reporting low rates, whereas high rates may serve as an indication of good reporting systems. Gender subgroups show a slight female predominance of rates in all countries which may require further study in the future.

Figure 2.19. Accidental puncture or laceration rates per 100 000 discharges, 2007

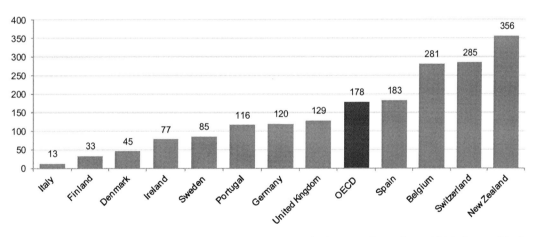

Note: Data for Denmark refer to 2008 and for Belgium and the United States, data refer to 2006. Cases with the critical incident present on hospital admission are excluded in the Canadian data.

Source: OECD Health Care Quality Database 2009.

While significant work in the development of these indicators has been invested over several pilot phases of the project, concerns remain regarding the true cause of the variations observed. In order to better understand patient safety across countries, having a valid measure is essential. Potential explanations for the fluctuations across countries include variation in:

- Discrepancies in hospital populations:

    - risk of injury or severity of illness (*i.e.*, countries with sicker patients may have higher PSI rates);

    - use of "short-stay" or "same-day surgery" services (*i.e.*, countries that treat healthier patients in ambulatory settings may have higher PSI rates, because only the sickest patients receive inpatient care);

    - length of stay and readmission patterns (*i.e.*, countries with shorter hospital stays may shift adverse events to readmissions).

- Discrepancies in electronic data systems and storage:

    - number of data fields collected and retained (*i.e.*, truncation of diagnoses may reduce reported PSI rates);

- Discrepancies in data collection:

    - medical classification systems (*i.e.*, ICD-9-CM versus ICD-10);

    - extent of secondary diagnosis coding based on physician documentation (*i.e.*, countries with better documentation and coding may have higher PSI rates);

    - other important elements in hospital administrative data are defined (*i.e.*, countries with better defined data elements may exclude more – or fewer – patients with adverse events).

As a result of careful follow-up work by the country representatives and the OECD Secretariat, several potential causes of variation can now be discounted. Age-sex standardisation was performed, based on an OECD standard hospitalised population, though this revealed very minor effects. Countries were asked to exclude "short-stay" or "same-day surgery" cases; when this was done, the apparent association (at the country level) between PSI rates and mean lengths of stay disappeared. It can be concluded that hospital populations are rather similar among participating countries.

Ongoing analytical work has revealed international differences in the definitions of key variables used for defining the at-risk population. Non-elective admission types show substantial and varying effects on the Postoperative sepsis indicator. As definitions and practices vary across countries, additional information should be sought to understand how acute and elective admissions are defined in each country. Furthermore, patient safety indicators with short length of stay (< 24h) exclusion have an effect of reducing bias, while longer length of stay exclusions (*e.g.* > four days) tend to increase bias. Collecting data for events by day breakdowns for length of stay may provide a better understanding of the effect of this exclusion. Possible revisions for this exclusion are likely to improve international comparability. Some countries reported that their data systems provide a limited number of data fields to store secondary diagnosis. These countries show significantly lower rates for all indicators, although there is still substantial variation among countries with robust data systems that include at least 12 diagnosis fields.

Variations in coding and medical classification systems are evident as some countries still use the Clinical Modification of ICD-9 whereas other countries use ICD-10 or modifications thereof. Despite this fact, no systematic effect of the classification system was found. Indicator definitions were provided in both ICD-9-CM as well as ICD-10. However, countries using earlier versions of ICD-9-CM reported calculation problems as some codes recently introduced by the United States to the ICD-9-CM are not available in the earlier versions used in those countries.

Depending on the purposes for which hospital administrative data are collected and used, the assignment of secondary diagnoses varies. In several countries, hospitals have no financial or regulatory incentives to code all documented diagnoses. In the 2008 and 2009 calculation projects, countries reported mean numbers of secondary diagnoses between 0.47 and 6.72 among hospitalised patients at risk. Countries reporting low mean numbers of secondary diagnoses showed systematically lower PSI rates in all three calculation rounds (Drösler *et al.*, 2009). On the other hand, countries reporting at least three secondary diagnoses on the average record showed more similar results, regardless which classification system was used. For example, Figure 2.20 shows the positive correlation across countries between the mean number of secondary diagnoses and the rate of Postoperative pulmonary embolism (PE) or deep vein thrombosis (DVT).

Figure 2.20. Positive correlation between the mean number of secondary diagnoses and the non-standardised rate of post-operative pulmonary embolism or deep vein thrombosis (n = 14)

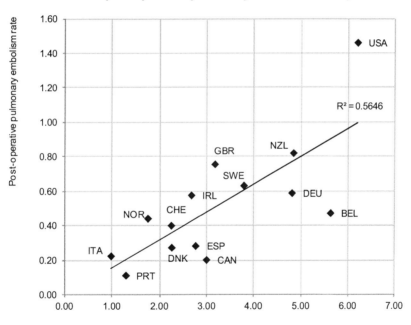

Source: *OECD Health Care Quality Database 2009.*

Some countries reported that no national coding guidelines are in use. Those countries may not have PSI rates that are comparable to those from countries with coding guidelines, because coding guidelines typically stipulate when a diagnosis should be coded (*i.e.,* based on physician documentation that the diagnosis affected the care of the patient during his or her stay in hospital).

Recent research on the validity of PSIs reveals that their validity is significantly improved by qualifying the timing of each secondary diagnosis (Utter *et al.*, 2009; White *et al.*, 2009). It is important to distinguish whether a secondary diagnosis was already present on hospital admission or developed during hospitalisation. Conditions that are present on hospital admission should not be counted as adverse events during hospitalisation. Some countries (*i.e.*, Canada, some US and Australian States) have added this qualifying secondary diagnosis marker to their data systems to improve the information content.

Often patients are hospitalised serially in different institutions. To improve information on patient safety events and to avoid double counting, anonymous tracking of patients in electronic data systems and linking safety information from multiple sources can support efforts in measuring quality.

Box 2.4. Quality and safety in Belgian hospitals

Since 2007, additional financing has been made available by the Federal Government (Federal Public Services – Public Health) to all Belgian hospitals that are willing to invest in the improvement of quality and patient safety. The project called "co-ordination of quality and patient safety" aims at the structural and long-term improvement of quality and patient safety in acute, psychiatric and long-term care hospitals and is defined as a multi-annual plan (2007-12). The project has been developed in response to both international movements on quality and patient safety, fostered by the Institute of Medicine reports, as well as to findings and research on quality and patient safety within Belgian hospitals.

During the first project year 80% of the Belgian hospitals signed up a contract with the Federal Government that specified the areas of improvement to be initiated and/or achieved within cycles of one year periods. During the first project year hospitals were asked to describe their mission, vision and strategy with regard to quality and patient safety as well as all related structures and functions. In addition hospitals were asked to perform the Hospital Survey on Patient Safety Culture (AHRQ), to report on (near) incidents and to describe three quality projects. The last part, which applied to acute hospitals only, included the selection of 12 quality indicators and the development of actions for improvement.

As from the second project year almost all hospitals (90%) subscribed to the project which then became structured around three basic pillars. These pillars follow the Donabedian triade of structure, process and outcome. The first pillar of the project targeted patient safety: hospitals were asked to develop a patient safety plan and to provide information on actions for improvement that resulted from the Hospital Survey on Patient Safety Culture. The second pillar of the project targeted processes. Hospitals were asked to invest in the analysis and improvement of mainly clinical processes. The third pillar was focusing on the use of indicators. Since 2008 hospitals gradually invested in the development of a multidimensional and integrated set of indicators.

Both the participation rate (maintained at 90%) and preliminary results of the project have shown that awareness has been raised in hospitals on the importance of quality and patient safety. Important features of the project are a mixed top-down/bottom-up approach, an intensive support of the participating hospitals by the Federal Government and the setting up of networks to exchange practices.

The Federal Government aims to implement the use of outcome data in the next multi-annual plan (2013-17) to allow for a more rigorous evaluation of quality and patient safety in Belgian hospitals.

Next steps and recommendations

The use of administrative hospital data to track patient safety across countries and over time has proven to be both practical and feasible. These data demonstrate considerable potential to improve patient safety in many OECD counties. Nevertheless, comparisons across countries have substantial room for improvement that could be achieved by the harmonisation of hospital data collection protocols and data systems:

- National coding standards, as many countries already use, should be introduced. Countries that are still using ICD-9-CM should switch to ICD-10 (or versions thereof), as ICD-9-CM will no longer be supported by the United States after 2013. At least 12 diagnosis fields should be collected per hospital stay and retained to avoid missing any important diagnoses and possible patient safety events.

- Hospitals should be encouraged to assign secondary diagnoses that are germane to the main diagnosis under treatment. This might be achieved through governmental oversight and payment mechanisms. Countries with insufficient numbers of hospital-reported diagnoses may have to be excluded from future comparisons as lower rates due to incomplete reporting or missing events can be misleading. Adjusting for the thoroughness of reporting may reduce bias in international comparisons, but is not an optimal solution to the problem.

- A qualifying marker to specify secondary diagnoses that were present on hospital admission should be added to country-specific data systems, as countries without this marker will incorrectly report higher PSI rates. This present on admission flag (currently employed in the United States and Canada) has shown good potential in helping identify patient safety events that result in re-admission.

- The introduction of a unique, encrypted patient identifier will allow more sophisticated methods of data analysis and facilitate future comparisons of health system performance.

2.7. Patient experience

Importance and relevance

Patients' insights into their health care experience can be invaluable when considering priorities for quality improvement in health care. Patient participation and feedback is important for national policy making (Van der Kraan, 2006), guideline development (Moreira, 2005; van de Bovenkamp and Trappenburg, 2009), and quality improvement (Bate and Robert, 2007) and scientific research and advice (Bal *et al.*, 2004; Epstein, 2008).

Various attempts to systematically measure patients' experience have been made over the past two decades. In the 1990s, patient satisfaction became an increasingly popular outcome measure in clinical trials. Patient satisfaction surveys were also increasingly used to elicit quality of care measures taken from the patients' perspective. In the mid-1990s, scholars began to argue that continuous quality improvement should be based on the underlying components of patient satisfaction *i.e.* expectation and experience (Sixma *et al.*, 1998). Since then, a number of new "families" of patient surveys have been developed. These focus not only on evaluating patient satisfaction but also on what actually happened to patients during their hospital stay or a visit to the doctor (Delnoij, 2009).

The reasons for studying patient experience differ across countries. The motives vary from promoting external accountability of health care providers to enhancing patient choice, or improving the quality of care. Countries also consider the quality of care perceived by patients as an integral part of health systems performance particularly after the publication of the WHO's *World Health Report 2000*. In addition, some countries have also begun to explore a possibility of utilising patient experience measurements to enhance integrated care in certain care models.

Currently several OECD countries undertake surveys to map the quality of care experienced by patients. In a number of countries, this is part of a systematic programme of work. According to a review commissioned by the OECD (Kunnskapssenteret, 2008), this is the case in Denmark, Norway, England, the Netherlands, Canada and the United States. Other countries such as the Czech Republic, Ireland, Japan, South Korea and Spain also conduct national work on patient experience measurement through hospitals, psychiatry and national surveys. In these countries, patient surveys are being standardised and in some instances patient experience information is used as a performance indicator of health care providers' quality. Box 2.5 provides an interesting example of how this has been achieved in the Czech Republic and Japan. In the United States, England and the Netherlands, patient experience data are used in pay-for-performance schemes.

Box 2.5. Development and use of patient experiences measurements: examples from countries

An increasing number of countries have developed methods of measuring patient experiences and utilised the data to improve health systems.

Czech Republic

The methodology for measuring patient experience has been developed since the 1990s. Over the past few years, it has become standardised through activities supported by the Ministry of Health. Research on patient experience methodologies, conducted in the Czech Republic has drawn from international experience. Furthermore, the country has been collecting patient experience data regularly through questionnaires for hospitals, rehabilitation facilities and psychiatric clinics. This work has focused on the eight quality dimensions developed by the Picker Institute (respecting a patient's values, preferences and expressed needs; information and education; access to care; emotional support; involvement of family and friends: continuity and transition; physical comfort; and co-ordination of care).

In 2008, a standard methodology was established for the analysis and reporting of the patient experience data. Since then health care performance has incorporated the use of patient experience information and this information has been reported in a comparative manner. Starting in 2010, the Ministry of Health has been also awarding "Satisfied Patient" certificates to the health care facilities with outstanding performance.

Japan

Patient experience surveys have been conducted every three years by the Japanese Ministry of Health, Labour and Welfare between 1996 and 2008. The purpose of this survey was initially to examine access to health care including transport fees as well as to examine actual patient experiences related to patient safety and openness of medical records as well as in communications with doctors and nurses and satisfaction with accommodation and meals. The subjects of these patient experience surveys are patients in ambulatory care and hospitalised patients. The questionnaires are delivered to randomly selected hospitals from all over Japan and obtained a high response rate: around 80% among more than 200 000 patients who took the survey.

In addition, the surveys are conducted along with other national surveys, such as patient survey and medical facilities survey. Although the patient experience survey itself is an anonymous survey about 30% of subjects could be linked to those different surveys which provide more detailed data on hospitals and disease coding. The internal consistency and reliability of a psychometric test score for a sample of examinees is assured about the questions of 2005 survey.

The recent 2008 survey assessed integrated and comprehensive care for patients, covering questions from access, experience in the hospital (ambulatory care and hospitalised care) through to care after they are discharged from the hospital. It contains questions on information provided to patients (for example on hospitals), waiting time and consulting time by doctors (ambulatory care), informed consent, patients' understanding of their health care as explained by health care professionals (doctors, nurses, etc.), communication with doctors and nurses, and general satisfaction.

The examples above illustrate that patient experience information is now widely accepted and used as a measure of health care quality. Measuring patient experience is a growing research industry in many OECD countries but these efforts tend to be country-specific and the measurements in one country tend not to be easily comparable with those for another.

International comparative research on patient experience is beginning to receive more attention. The Commonwealth Fund (CMWF), the Picker Institute Europe and the WHO have all engaged in international comparisons of patients' experience but a stable and reliable international instrument to measure patient experience is not yet available.

In this context, in 2007, OECD member countries endorsed plans to develop internationally comparable measures of patients' experience as part of the Health Care Quality Indicators Project. In addition, a patient experience expert subgroup was established to oversee and advise on ongoing and future development work. The number of countries currently participating in the subgroup is 23 (21 OECD and two non-OECD countries).

As part of the development process for the cross-country comparison instrument referred to above, it was decided to develop a pilot patient experience questionnaire. The purpose of the pilot was test the relevance of some of the key dimension of quality and to test the suitability of the questionnaire with participating countries. It was also decided to test the relevance and applicability of the questionnaire in different health systems and to assess its psychometric properties.

In developing the pilot questionnaire, the following principles were considered:

- Suitability for international use, *i.e.* it should consist, as far as possible, of generic, system-independent questions;

- Temporal stability, *i.e.* questions should be independent of contemporary policy priorities;

- Multilingual design;

- Multipurpose design, *i.e.* it should be usable as a stand-alone questionnaire or for integration with other instruments;

- Multi-model design, *i.e.* suitable for use for telephone/face to face/other survey methods.

Following consultation with the expert group and others and drawing on methodologies from other validated questionnaires, the pilot OECD Patient Experience Questionnaire was developed. The pilot questionnaire was designed to elicit the experiences of patients aged 18 and over who had had contact with ambulatory care over the past 12 months. The domains of particular interest were access, communication and autonomy.

Patient experience is difficult to measure. People's perception about the care they receive is influenced by many things such as expectations based on the design or stated purpose of the health system in question. Individual traits, attitudes to health and social and economic class also come into play. These factors and many others contribute to the complexity in measuring and interpreting data on patient experience within and across countries. In order to improve the cross-country comparability of patient experiences, vignettes have been used recently in international surveys conducted by different agencies including WHO (Box 2.6), but it is considered that the instrument is not yet mature enough for its use in the pilot questionnaire.

Box 2.6. What are vignettes?

Vignettes are fictitious short stories on a fictional person's experiences of health systems. Responses following vignettes are used to anchor the survey respondent's responses on his/her own experiences of the system. An example of a vignette from the WHO's Health Survey 2002 in autonomy is provided below.

Autonomy

[Mark] had a serious health problem. The doctor prescribed the best treatment for [Mark] but without telling him the implications on his quality of life or the cost. [Mark] felt powerless and was not given any information to help him to feel more in control.

Q7507 How would you rate [Mark's] experience of getting information about other types of treatments or tests?

1. Very good, 2. Good, 3. Moderate, 4. Bad, 5. Very bad.

Q7508 How would you rate [Mark's] experience of being involved in making decisions about his health care or treatment?

1. Very good, 2. Good, 3. Moderate, 4. Bad, 5. Very bad.

Several studies have been conducted in this area and recent studies include the one evaluating the validity of vignette approaches in the World Health Survey (Rice *et al.*, 2009a) and the other by the same authors (Rice *et al.*, 2009b) illustrating the differences in the ranking of health system responsiveness with and without vignettes anchoring adjustments.

Next steps

The following steps are foreseen in the further development of international comparable instruments for measuring patient experiences:

Administrating pilot data collection

A pilot questionnaire was field tested in conjunction with the 2010 population-based survey of the Commonwealth Fund (CMWF). Based on the consultation with CMWF, it was agreed to include 17 out of 22 questions from the HCQI questionnaire in their 2010 survey.

Participating countries administered the data collection in different ways – either through the Commonwealth Fund Health Care Quality Survey 2010 or via a country-specific survey. Eleven OECD countries participated in the Commonwealth Fund Survey 2010. In addition, ten countries expressed interest in participating in the activities around further testing of the pilot questionnaire proposed by the OECD.

Translating the pilot questionnaire

International questionnaires require appropriate translation in order to ensure that responses are elicited in a consistent manner and not biased by translational misinterpretation. Translation protocols have been developed by agencies conducing international surveys including CWF and ARHQ. Participating countries, collecting data through their own surveys and conducting cognitive testing, translate the questionnaire in their own languages, following international protocols.

Undertaking cognitive testing

Cognitive testing is generally conducted, to evaluate if questionnaire items, response options and instructions are clear, and easy to understand. The evaluation of cognitive testing is useful for fine-tuning purposes. The initial questionnaire was tested on 25 international students at the Erasmus University in the Netherlands in August, 2009. Feedback from the students was used to refine the questionnaire.

Evaluating psychometric properties

Psychometric analysis will be conducted to assess the validity (measuring what it is designed to measure) and the reliability (measuring consistently) of the pilot questionnaire. The overarching reason for this assessment is to ensure that the results of the survey are fit for international comparison purposes. Psychometric analysis using data collected in the Czech Republic showed that the pilot OECD questionnaire had good construct validity and high internal consistency.

Planning future data collection

Feedback from the experts and participating countries experience in the pilot phase will be used to identify further issues for evaluation or development.

Key lessons and recommendations: principles for national systems of patient experiences measurement

When a country aims to set up a national system for the measurement of patient experience, initiatives elsewhere can provide guidance on the underlying key principles. Based on experience in this field as discussed in OECD's Health Care Quality Indicator Project , several guiding principles have emerged which may be interest to others embarking on similar work. Box 2.7 provides a synopsis of these.

Box 2.7. Principles for establishing national systems of patient experiences proposed by the HCQI Project

Principle 1. Patient measurement should be patient-based

Patient experience survey instruments should be formulated with the input of patients themselves. This can be done through focus groups or interviews of representative patient groups. Doing so will ensure that issues included in the survey are relevant and important. It is also useful to assess the relative importance of the priority areas that have been identified. Items included in the survey should reflect "demand" side characteristics rather than need "need" side characteristics. Finally, for the measured results to be taken seriously it is important that the institution(s) in charge of the work have public credibility.

Principle 2. The goals of patient measurement should be clear

Patient measures can be used for a variety of goals. Some systems are set up for "external" reasons such as the provision of consumer information to increase patient choice, accountability towards the general public on performance or as information used by financiers in pay-for-performance schemes. Other initiatives have more "internal" goals such as quality improvement by the providers. Although specific measures can be used for various goals, it is important to be explicit about the goals before developing the measurements. For example, if the goal is quality improvement, the instrument should deal with the actionable aspects of the care delivery process. By doing so the results will be tailored in such a way so as to enable health care providers to learn lessons and improve. When the goal is to facilitate choice, the measures should be able to show meaningful differences between health care providers.

Principle 3. Patient measurement tools should undergo cognitive testing and the psychometric properties should be known

Like all indicators, patient measurement tools such as surveys should meet the basic scientific criteria of validity. Documentation should exist on the testing of the tools, including the results of cognitive testing (*e.g.* assuring correct and consistent interpretation of the questions) and the psychometric properties (*e.g.* assuring that the items used in the questionnaire actually measure the constructs they pertain to measure). Changes in questionnaires should be documented and when necessary re-tested.

Principle 4. The actual measurement and analyses of patient experiences should be standardised

The methodology of patient experience measurement does not only apply to the development of measurement tools but also to the actual measurement (*e.g.* via mail survey, telephone survey, structured interview), the analyses of data and the reporting. To ensure reliability, the data collection methods and analyses must be standardised and reproducible. Several countries working with systematic measurement of patient experiences have introduced accreditation procedures for the various agencies/vendors who conduct surveys.

Principle 5. The reporting method of findings of patient experiences measurement should be chosen with care

In presenting the results of patient experience measurement there is always a tension between presenting a clear and easy-to-understand message and the methodological limitations of drawing certain conclusions. There is a good deal of literature is available on the reporting of patient experience information, and this body of knowledge should be taken into account when choosing a particular reporting format.

Principle 6. International comparability of measurement of patient experiences should be enhanced

Methodological efforts by countries to develop and use systematic ways of measuring patient experience information are diverse and plentiful. Experience indicates that countries are keen to copy and adjust questions and questionnaires applied elsewhere. Give the OECDs work in this field and its position as a central broker of quality improvement initiatives, it is ideally placed to facilitate shared learning of national experiences in this regard. To this end, the HCQI Project will continue to act as a repository and disseminating centre for patient experience expertise.

Principle 7. National systems for the measurement of patient experiences should be sustainable

A national system for the measurement of patient experience should monitor trends longitudinally. This requires long term health system commitment and resourcing. Therefore, sustainability of the organisational and research and development infrastructure is an important condition for its success.

Bibliography

Ackroyd-Stolarz, S., J. Guernsey, N. MacKinnon and G. Kovacs (2009), "Impact of Adverse Events on Hospital Disposition in Community-Dwelling Seniors Admitted to Acute Care", *Health Care Quarterly*, pp. 34-39.

Arah, O.A., G. Westert *et al.* (2006), "A Conceptual Framework for the OECD Health Care Quality Indicators Project", *International Journal of Health Care Quality*, Vol. 18, Suppl. 1, pp. 5-13.

Bal, R., W. Bijker *et al.* (2004), "Democratisation of Scientific Advice", *British Medical Journal*, Vol. 329, No. 7478, pp. 1339-1341.

Bate, P. and G. Robert (2007), *Experience-based Design: From Redesigning the System Around the Patient to Co-designing Services with the Patient*, Radcliffe Publishing, Abingdon.

Brady, A., R. Redmond *et al.* (2009), "Adverse Events in Health Care: A Literature Review", *Journal of Nursing Management*, Vol. 17, No. 2, pp. 155-164.

Brennan, T., L. Leape *et al.* (2004), "Incidence of Adverse Events and Negligence in Hospitalized Patients: Results of the Harvard Medical Practice Study I 1991", *Quality and Safety in Health Care*, Vol. 13, No. 2, pp. 145-151.

Brown, M., G. Riley, N. Schussler and R. Etzioni (2002), "Estimating Health Care Costs Related to Cancer Treatment from SEER-Medicare Data", *Medical Care*, Vol. 40, No. 8, Suppl IV, pp. 104-117.

Capewell, S., J. Pell, C. Morrison and J. McMurray (1999), "Increasing the Impact of Cardiological Treatments. How Best to Reduce Deaths", *European Heart Journal*, Vol. 20, No. 19, pp. 1386-1392.

Care Quality Commission (2009), "National Study Closing the Gap Tackling Cardiovascular Disease and Health Inequalities by Prescribing Statins and Stop Smoking Services".

CCCG (2000), "Palliative Chemotherapy for Advanced Colorectal Cancer: Systematic Review and Meta-Analysis by the Colorectal Cancer Collaborative Group", *British Medical Journal*, Vol. 321, No. 7260, pp. 531-535.

Checkland, K. (2007), "Understanding General Practice: A Conceptual Framework Developed from Case Studies in the UK NHS", *British Journal of General Practice*, Vol. 57, No. 534, pp. 56-63.

de Vries, E., M. Ramrattan *et al.* (2008), "The Incidence and Nature of In-hospital Adverse Events: A Systematic Review", *Quality and Safety in Health Care*, Vol. 17, No. 3, pp. 216-223.

Delnoij, D. (2009), "Measuring Patient Experiences in Europe: What Can We Learn from the Experiences in the USA and England?", *European Journal of Public Health*, Vol. 19, No. 4, pp. 354-356.

Davila, R.E., E. Rajan, T.H. Baron, D.G. Adler *et al.* (2006), "Standards of Practice Committee, American Society for Gastrointestinal. ASGE Guideline: Colorectal Cancer Screening and Surveillance", *Gastrointestinal Endoscopy*, Vol. 63, No. 4, pp. 546-557.

Drösler, S., N. Klazinga *et al.* (2009), "Application of Patient Safety Indicators Internationally: A Pilot Study Among Seven Countries", *International Journal for Quality in Health Care*, Vol. 21, No. 4, pp. 272-278.

Eaton, W., S. Martins *et al.* (2008), "The Burden of Mental Disorders", *Epidemiologic Reviews*, Vol. 30, pp. 1-14.

Epstein, S. (2008), *Patient Groups and Health Movements*, MIT Press, Cambridge.

Faivre-Finn, C., A. Bouvier, E. Mitry, E. Rassiat, F. Clinard and J. Faivre (2002), "Chemotherapy for Colon Cancer in a Well-defined French Population: Is It Under- or Over-prescribed?, *Aliment Pharmacology and Therapeutics*, Vol. 16, No. 3, pp. 353-359.

Fajutrao, L., J. Locklear, J. Priaulx and A. Heyes (2009), "A Systematic Review of the Evidence of the Burden of Bipolar Disorder in Europe", *Clinical Practice and Epidemiology in Mental Health*, Vol. 9, No. 5:3, *DOI:10.1186/1745-0179.*

Ferlay, .J, D.M. Parkin and E. Steliarova-Foucher (2010), "GLOBOCAN 2008, Cancer Incidence and Mortality Worldwide", *IARC Cancer Base*, No. 10, Lyon, France, available from: *http://globocan.iarc.fr.*

Fox, M., S. Mealing, R. Anderson, J. Dean, K. Stein, A. Price *et al.* (2007), "The Clinical Effectiveness and Cost-effectiveness of Cardiac Resynchronisation (Biventricular Pacing) for Heart Failure: Systematic Review and Economic Model", *Health Technology Assessment*, Vol. 11, No. 47, pp. iii-iv, ix-248.

Garcia-Armesto, S., H. Medeiros and L. Wei (2008), "Information Availability for Measuring and Comparing Quality of Mental Health Care Across OECD Countries", OECD Health Technical Paper No. 20, OECD Publishing, Paris.

Gatta, G., M. Lasota and A. Verdecchia (1998), "Survival of European Women with Gynaecological Tumours, During the Period 1978-1989", *European Journal of Cancer*, Vol. 34, No. 14, pp. 2218-2225.

Gil, V. (1999), "Right Ventricular Dysfunction in Left Dysfunction Caused by Ischemia: Conditioning Factors and Implications", *Revista Portuguesa de Cardiologia*, Vol. 18, No. 12, pp. 1163-1172.

Goldberg, R., J. Gurwitz and J. Gore (1999), "Duration of, and Temporal Trends (1994-1997) in, Prehospital Delay in Patients with Acute Myocardial Infarction: The second National Registry of Myocardial Infarction", *Archives of Internal Medicine*, Vol. 159, No. 18, pp. 2141-2147.

Govindarajan, A., N. Coburn, A. Kiss, L. Rabeneck, A. Smith and C. Law (2006), "Population-based Assessment of the Surgical Management of Locally Advanced Colorectal Cancer", *Journal of National Cancer Institute*, Vol. 98, No. 20, pp. 474-481.

Granados, D., A. Lefranc *et al.* (2005), "Disability-adjusted Life Years: An Instrument for Defining Public Health Priorities?, *Revue d'Epidemiologie et de Santé Publique*, Vol. 53, No. 2, pp. 111-125.

Harper, D., E. Franco, C. Wheeler and A. Moscicki (2006), "HPV Vaccine Study Group. Sustained Efficacy Up to 4.5 Years of a Bivalent L1 Virus-like Particle Vaccine Against Human Papillomavirus Types 16 and 18: Follow-up from a Randomised Control Trial", *The Lancet*, Vol. 367, No. 9518, pp. 1247-1255.

Hermann, R., S. Mattke *et al.* (2006), "Quality Indicators for International Benchmarking of Mental Health Care", *International Journal for Quality in Health Care*, Vol. 18, Suppl. 1, pp. 31-38.

Institute of Medicine (2005), *Improving the Quality of Health Care for Mental and Substance-Use Conditions: Quality Chasm Series*, released Nov. 1, 2005, National Academy Press, Washington D.C.

Johnston, K., W. Westerfield *et al.* (2009), "The Direct and Indirect Costs of Employee Depression, Anxiety, and Emotional Disorders – An Employer Case Study", *Journal of Occupational and Environmental Medicine*, Vol. 51, No. 5, pp. 564-577.

Kastrup, M. and A. Ramos (2007), "Global Mental Health", *Danish Medical Bulletin*, Vol. 54, No. 1, pp. 42-43.

Khush, K., E. Rapaport and D. Waters (2005), "The History of the Coronary Care Unit", *Canadian Journal of Cardiology*, Vol. 21, No. 12, pp. 1041-1045.

Kilbourne, A., D. Greenwald *et al.* (2010), "Financial Incentives and Accountability for Integrated Medical Care in Department of Veterans Affairs Mental Health Programs", *Psychiatric Services*, Vol. 61, No. 1, pp. 38-44.

Knapp, M., R. Mangalore *et al.* (2004), "The Global Costs of Schizophrenia", *Schizophrenia Bulletin*, Vol. 30, No. 2, pp. 279-293.

Kohn, L. and M. Donaldson (2000), *To Err Is Human: Building a Safer Health System*, Institute of Medicine.

Kringos, D., W. Boerma *et al.* (2010), "The Breadth of Primary Care: A Systematic Literature Review of Its Core Dimensions", *BMC Health Services Research*, Vol. 10, No. 65.

Kunnskapssenteret (2008), *National and Cross-national Surveys of Patient Experiences: A Structured Review*, Norwegian Knowledge Centre for the Health Services.

Lien, L. (2002), "Trends in International Health Development", *World Hospitals and Health Services*, Vol. 38, No. 2, pp. 31-35.

Loveland, A. (2008), "Using Patient Safety Indicators to Estimate the Impact of Potential Adverse Events on Outcomes", *Medical Care Research and Review*, pp. 65-67.

Loveland, A., P. Romano and A. Rosen (2008), "Using Patient Safety Indicators to Estimate the Impact of Potential Adverse Events on Outcomes", *Medical Care Research and Review*, pp. 65-67.

Marshall, M., N. Klazinga *et al.* (2006), "OECD Health Care Quality Indicator Project. The Expert Panel on Primary Care Prevention and Health Promotion", *International Journal for Quality in Health Care*, Vol. 18, Suppl. 1, pp. 21-25.

Mathers, C., D. Fat, M. Inoue, C. Rao and A. Lopez (2005), "Counting the Dead and What They Died From: An Assessment of the Global Status of Cause of Death Data", *Bulletin of the World Health Organization*, Vol. 83, No. 3, pp. 171-177.

Mattke, S., A. Epstein *et al.* (2006), "The OECD Health Care Quality Indicators Project: History and Background", *International Journal for Quality in Health Care*, Vol. 18, Suppl. 1, pp. 1-4.

Mauri, D., N. Polyzos, G. Salanti, N. Pavlidis and J. Ioannidis (2008), "Multiple-treatments Meta-analysis of Chemotherapy and Targeted Therapies in Advanced Breast Cancer", *Journal of the National Cancer Institute*, Vol. 100, No. 24, pp. 1780-1791.

McDonald, R., S. Campbell *et al.* (2009), "Practice Nurses and the Effects of the New General Practitioner Contract in the English National Health Service: The Extension of a Professional Project?", *Social Science and Medicine*, Vol. 68, No. 7, pp. 1206-1212.

McGovern, P., D.J. Jacobs, E. Shahar, D. Arnett, A. Folsom, H. Blackburn *et al.* (2001), "Trends in Acute Coronary Heart Disease Mortality, Morbidity, and Medical Care from 1985 through 1997: The Minnesota Heart Survey", *Circulation*, Vol. 104, No. 1, pp. 19-24.

McLoughlin, V., J. Millar *et al.* (2006), "Selecting Indicators for Patient Safety at the Health System Level in OECD Countries", *International Journal for Quality in Health Care*, Vol. 18, Suppl. 1, pp. 14-20.

Midgley, R. and D. Kerr (1999), "Colorectal Cancer", *The Lancet*, Vol. 353, No. 9150, pp. 391-399.

Moreira, T. (2005), "Diversity in Clinical Guidelines: The Role of Repertoires of Evaluation", *Social Science and Medicine*, Vol. 60, No. 9, pp. 1975-1985.

OECD (2003), *A Disease-based Comparison of Health Systems: What Is Best and at What Cost?*, OECD Publishing, Paris

OECD (2010a), *Improving Health Sector Efficiency: The Role of Information and Communication Technologies*, OECD Publishing, Paris.

OECD (2010b), *Sickness, Disability and Work: A Synthesis of Findings for OECD Countries*, OECD Publishing, Paris.

Prince, M., V. Patel *et al.* (2007), "No Health Wthout Mental Health", *The Lancet*, Vol. 370, No. 9590, pp. 859-877.

Quan, D., V. Sundararajan, E. Wen, B. Burnand *et al.* (2008), "Adaptation of AHRQ Patient Safety Indicators for Use in ICD-10 Administrative Data by an International Consortium. Advances in Patient Safety", Agency for Healthcare Research and Quality, Rockville, MD.

Rice, N., S. Robone and P. Smith (2009a), "Vignettes and Health Systems Responsiveness in Crosscountry Comparative Analyses", Health, Econometrics and Data Group (HEDG) Working Paper No. 09/29, HEDG, Department of Economics, University of York.

Rice, N., S. Robone and P. Smith (2009b), "Analysis of the Validity of the Vignette Approach to Correct for Heterogeneity in Reporting Health System Responsiveness",

Health, Econometrics and Data Group (HEDG) Working Paper No. 09/28, HEDG, Department of Economics, University of York.

Rossler, W., H. Salize *et al.* (2005), "Size of Burden of Schizophrenia and Psychotic Disorders", *European Neuropsychopharmacology*, Vol. 15, No. 4, pp. 399-409.

Sant, M., C. Allemani, M. Santaquilani, A. Knijn, F. Marchesi, R. Capocaccia *et al.* (2009), "EUROCARE-4. Survival of Cancer Patients Diagnosed in 1995-1999. Results and Commentary", *European Journal of Cancer*, Vol. 45, No. 6, pp. 931-991.

SEER – Surveillance, Epidemiology, and End Results (2009), *Cancer Statistics Review 1975-2007*, Retrieved from National Cancer Institute: *http://seer.cancer.gov /csr/1975_2007/*.

Serretti, A., L. Mandelli *et al.* (2009), "The Socio-economical Burden of Schizophrenia: A Simulation of Cost-offset of Early Intervention Program in Italy", *European Psychiatry*, Vol. 24, No. 1, pp. 11-16.

Sixma, H., J. Kerssens *et al.* (1998), "Quality of Care from the Patients' Perspective: From Theoretical Concept to a New Measuring Instrument", *Health Expectations*, Vol. 1, No. 2, pp. 82-95.

Starfield, B., L. Shi *et al.* (2005), "Contribution of Primary Care to Health Systems and Health", *Milbank Quarterly*, Vol. 83, No. 3, pp. 457-502.

Sutton, M. and G. McLean (2006), "Determinants of Primary Medical Care Quality Measured Under the New United Kingdom Contract: Cross Sectional Study", *British Medical Journal*, Vol. 332, No. 7538, pp. 389-390.

Tu, J., L. Nardi, J. Fang, J. Liu, L. Khalid, H. Johansen *et al.* (2009), "National Trends in Rates of Death and Hospital Admissions Related to Acute Myocardial Infarction, Heart Failure and Stroke, 1994-2004", *Canadian Medical Association Journal*, Vol. 180, No. 13, pp. e118-e125.

USPSTF – U.S. Preventive Services Task Force (2009), "Screening for Breast Cancer: U.S. Preventive Services Task Force Recommendation Statement", *Annals of Internal Medicine*, Vol. 151, No. 10, pp. 716-726, W-236.

Utter, G., P. Zrelak *et al.* (2009), "Positive Predictive Value of the AHRQ Accidental Puncture or Laceration Patient Safety Indicator", *Annals of Surgery*, Vol. 250, No. 6, pp. 1041-1045.

Valladares, A., T. Dilla *et al.* (2009), "Depression: A Social Mortgage. Latest Advances in Knowledge of the Cost of the Disease", *Actas Espanolas de Psiquiatria*, Vol. 37, No. 1, pp. 49-53.

van de Bovenkamp, H. and M.J. Trappenburg (2009), "Reconsidering Patient Participation in Guideline Development", *Health Care Analysis*, Vol. 17, No. 3, pp. 198-216.

van der Kraan, W. (2006), "Vraag naar vraagsturing. Een verkennend onderzoek naar de betekenis van vraagsturing in de Nederlandse gezondheidszorg, iBMG", PhD-thesis, Erasmus Universiteit, Rotterdam.

Verdecchia, A., S. Francisci, H. Brenner, G. Gatta, A. Micheli, L. Mangone *et al.* (2007), "Recent Cancer Survival in Europe: A 2000-02 Period Analysis of EUROCARE-4 Data", *The Lancet Oncology*, Vol. 8, No. 9, pp. 784-796.

Weisfeldt, M. and S. Zieman (2007), "Advances in the Prevention and Treatment of Cardiovascular Disease", *Health Affairs (Millwood)*, Vol. 26, No. 1, pp. 25-37.

White, R., B. Sadeghi *et al.* (2009), "How Valid is the ICD-9-CM Based AHRQ Patient Safety Indicator for Postoperative Venous Thromboembolism?", *Medical Care*, Vol. 47, No. 12, pp. 1237-1243.

WHO – World Health Organization (2001), *The World Health Report 2001 – Mental Health: New Understanding, New Hope*, WHO, Geneva.

Chapter 3

How Can National Health Information Infrastructures Improve the Measurement of Quality of Care?

Good information on health care quality requires systematic data collection and reporting capabilities. The following section reviews current state of health information systems and the challenges associated with their development.

Policy makers are keen to introduce measures to improve quality. However, their good intentions are often hampered by the lack of data or its poor quality often arising from a failure to link records across institutions. The previous chapters have described the conceptual, methodological and operational challenges associated with constructing and measuring indicators of quality of care. Difficulties in the calculation of internationally comparable quality indicators arise due to a number of reasons – slow adoption of electronic health records; the lack of unique patient identifiers and system-wide data linkage; lack of nationally-representative data, and differences in coding systems and data collection practices and sources.

Moreover, international comparisons, including those used in the HCQI Project, face the challenge of definitional differences in, methods, data, and reporting periods. HCQI's work has revealed valuable insights on the barriers and obstacles relating to data collection and interpretation. The work has also highlighted key issues that must be considered when developing indicators and mechanisms for inter-country quality monitoring purposes.

In this chapter, we describe the main sources of data for monitoring quality of care and we discuss their respective strengths and weaknesses. Additionally, examples are provided of national policies that are aimed at improving data availability. The chapter also describes continuing HCQI work that can be used to enhance national information infrastructures.

3.1.   Reviewing developments in national health information infrastructures

The need to modernise health information infrastructures has been emphasised in this report. If health care quality is to be taken seriously, it requires good quality data to monitor it. In turn, good quality data that covers the gamut of increasingly complex health care processes requires effective information architecture to collect it. For example, following discussions with country experts and a survey, designed to assess the information potential of health systems, it was concluded that information systems were insufficiently developed to collect data for comparative purposes for primary and mental health care.

With respect to patient safety and indicators on preventable admissions, it is noteworthy that the HCQI Project increasingly relies on administrative databases, such as hospital information systems. Experience in using these data repositories has provided valuable insights regarding their shortcomings. Table 3.1 below provides a summary of the key issues.

In order improve the problems with information infrastructures, it is important to understand the limitations of the data sources currently used for generating data for population-based quality indicators.

In the next section we identify the key data sources and we reflect on their limitations. The section also discusses how these issues relate to the ICT health agenda more broadly and to electronic health records (EHRs) more specifically. We also explore the prerequisites for linking data sources by means of unique patient identifiers (UPIs).

Table 3.1. Problems associated with generating internationally comparable quality indicators

Primary care	Data infrastructure is severely lacking in most countries National databases are not developed or comparable for data collection and comparison Coding is based on diseases and guidelines, rather than patients Coding practices are highly influenced by reimbursement
Acute care	Poor quality of coding practices for administrative databases, mostly using the outdated ICD-9 classification system (focus on diseases rather than patients) Lack of internationally-standardised procedure codes Lack of secondary-diagnosis coding Lack of present-on-admission coding Lack of data linkage, *e.g.* via unique patient identifiers Electronic health records are not well developed
Mental health care	Lack of data infrastructure to track patients across care settings, *e.g.* via unique patient identifiers Lack of comparable measures of outcomes across countries
Cancer care	Lack of national representativeness – cancer registries do not cover the entire population Cancer staging data are not available in most countries Data linkages between cancer registries and administrative databases (*e.g.* hospitals) are lacking
Patient safety	Lack of electronic health records Poor quality of medical records Lack of secondary diagnoses in administrative data systems Lack of present-on-admission flags in administrative databases (*e.g.* infections and bed sores) Data linkage within hospitals (*i.e.* laboratory or pharmacy) or outside hospitals (*i.e.* primary care) is lacking
Patient experience	Lack of nationally-standardised measurement systems of patient experience

3.2. The five main types of information sources for population-based quality indicators

Five main types of information source are currently used in the construction of population-based quality indicators:

- Birth and death statistics (mortality data);

- Specific registries (*i.e.* data on cancer, communicable diseases, specific diseases and specialties such as hip-replacement or surgical complications);

- Administrative databases;

- Electronic health records;

- Population and patient-based surveys (*i.e.* responsiveness).

Birth and death statistics

Birth and death statistics are available in all OECD countries and are the oldest data source for international comparative studies. Overall, the administrative systems to register birth and death are complete and robust – with cause of death data being coded in an internationally comparable way.

However, one of the main limitations with death data is the lack of secondary diagnoses. For example, when considering mental health care quality, it would be relevant to compare excess mortality rates for persons diagnosed with schizophrenia or bipolar-disorder (average life-expectancy in this instance is serving as a proxy measure for the quality of mental health). However, death data without secondary diagnosis coding, may underestimate the number of people dying with a diagnosis of interest – in this instance severe mental health.

Unique patient identifiers (UPIs) can help resolve such problems by facilitating linkage between death registries and other potentially relevant administrative databases (*e.g.* hospital information systems). By linking data sources by means of a UPI we can supplement information deficits in the primary source (death registry) with data found in the secondary source.

National registries

The HCQI Project relies heavily on national registries in such areas as communicable diseases and cancer. Several countries have implemented disease (*i.e.* diabetes) or specialty specific (*i.e.* surgery) registries and these are useful sources for information on quality of care. A good example of the way in which such data can be put to use for quality monitoring purposes at the local level is discussed in Box 3.1. Apart from coverage limitations, the international comparability of registry data is hampered by coding differences.

**Box 3.1. Best Information through Regional Outcomes (BIRO):
a European model for the automatic production
of standardised quality indicators in diabetes**

The regular production and update of quality indicators at the international level requires sustainable solutions for performance reporting within and across countries. Risk adjustment poses the problem of making large sets of microdata available at the international level, while data protection laws increasingly limit the secondary use of sensitive data. The EU BIRO/EUBIROD Consortia (2005-11) developed a general solution for the production of risk adjusted performance indicators. Structured processing of resident data leaves exclusive access and full control to local administrators. Client software maps local definitions to EU standards and runs statistical procedures to deliver fully standardised "local" descriptive reports. Aggregate data resulting from the calculation of on-site indicators ("statistical objects") are transmitted towards a central repository, which maintains and runs server software to produce European "global" reports for 72 indicators on diabetes. Multivariate logistic regression techniques are employed to produce risk adjusted indicators using the AHRQ methodology on top of finely tuned aggregated data. The architecture has been validated against principles of the EU Data Protection Directive through a formal process of privacy impact assessment. The model is completely open source (Java, PostgreSQL, R, Latex) and packaged into a multi-platform distribution running on Windows/Linux.

Administrative databases

In many countries, administrative data and databases are being increasingly used for quality monitoring purposes. Typically, these repositories contain data extracted from claims, billing/payment data, vital records, service utilisation, census data, and other sources. More often than not however, these databases lack important patient care information such as physical examination and laboratory results etc. Notwithstanding these shortfalls, there are distinct advantages to accessing administrative data for quality monitoring purposes. They often cover a wide range of patient services – outpatient and inpatient care, prescribing, etc. Data from administrative sources are typically inexpensive and accessible. They are also likely to be contemporary – a distinct advantage when measuring quality or when seeking to assess the impact of health policy.

For the HCQI Project the use of information derived from administrative data bases is vital. New indicators relating to hospital re-admission (mental health care), potentially preventable admissions (primary care, health promotion and prevention), and patient safety indicators (PSIs) are predominantly sourced from administrative databases.

Electronic health records

OECD countries are adopting health information and communication technologies (ICTs) as a tool for streamlining health care information feeds and processes. These developments are vital in order to keep pace with an increasingly complex array of information feeds arising from more complex and multidimensional care processes. Electronic health record (EHR) systems are now an essential component for health systems that are serious about pursuing quality, cost savings, and efficient and safe care processes. In New Zealand for example, widespread screening of adults ages 45 and over for cardiovascular disease now takes place using an automated web-based risk assessment tool. Although these data are being collected solely for clinical management purposes, they also yield a high dividend for population health monitoring and health care performance measurement.

Provided ongoing problems with EHRs development are resolved (inclusion of unstructured and uncodified text, lack of standardisation, etc.), their potential for quality monitoring purposes are huge.

Population surveys

Most OECD countries today carry out a range of population health surveys covering a range of topics including health status, living standards, drug use, prevalence of specific diseases etc. Often these surveys are longitudinal and span multiple years thereby providing valuable information on health and health related trends. Survey data are primarily collected through mail, telephone or personal interviews. Individual level surveys carried out to study for population health variations, are typically completed at national or sub national levels. Notable drawbacks in the use of surveys include their expense, they are methodologically demanding and their reliability for certain types of conditions can be questionable.

For some of its indicators, the HCQI Project uses data collected through surveys and reported via OECD's Health Data. As discussed in Chapter 2, Section 2.7, we are also considering the potential to harmonise the use of surveys to systematically assess patient experience across OECD countries.

3.3. Synthesising the lessons learned

Box 3.2 provides a summary of the lessons and insights gained from HCQI's work using all five data sources:

Box 3.2. Summary of lessons learned

Controlling for differences in population structures across countries

Without age-standardisation, countries may appear to be performing better (or worse) than they actually are, because they have younger (or older) population structures. Adjusting for age is therefore undertaken for most HCQI indicators, this can in turn, cause its own problems when, for example, the reference population used becomes dated with time.

Controlling variability of data sources

Data often come from different sources in different countries and are collected for different purposes.. For example, registries for prevention activities such as vaccination often do not cover settings outside the health care system *e.g.* community centres, private organisations and local campaigns. Therefore there is a risk of underestimation of the rates.

Identifying nationally representative data

Sometimes data on cancer survival rates, AMI case fatality rates and diabetes care process indicators are only available for a part of a country. In these instances it is important qualify the extent to which the region that is used is representative of the country as a whole.

Determining the retrospective completeness of the time series

Almost all international comparative efforts face problems in obtaining continuous, reliable data over time. This limits the ability to conduct meaningful trend analysis.

Adjusting for differences in ability to track individual patients (unique patient identifiers)

The most efficient utility to facilitate patient-based calculations is the unique patient identifier (UPIs). Using a unique code, patients can be tracked throughout the health system, thereby linking their care journey across disparate institutions. UPIs also enable the efficient construction of outcome measures such as post treatment mortality monitoring. For example, the ability to identify a fatal outcome within the 30 days following an episode of AMI or stroke, once the patient has left the hospital, is much higher when the patient can be identified, independently of where they are treated.

Improving data linkage

In order to gain a complete picture of the health care quality and safety of care, health data stored in disparate care/care related settings needs to be linked, preferably at the individual patient level. In this context, the implementation of unique patient identifiers is deemed useful for all countries. Demands to improve data infrastructure must be balanced with the demands for good epidemiological practice, confidentiality and privacy. Accordingly, countries need to develop guideline recommendations, standard operating procedures and pilot studies to build a suitable and sound framework for improving quality of care data infrastructure.

Improving measures

HCQI work in primary care, patient safety and mental health has highlighted the changing nature of population health and the increasing importance of capturing information on co-morbidity. In recognising these changing needs it is apparent that patient-level data that incorporates information about their complications and comorbidities, is now a pressing requirement. Thus the emphasis needs to shift from disease-based quality measures towards measures that are patient-based.

Improving consistent coding practices

There are outstanding issues concerning variation in documentation and coding practices across countries. The absence of consensus on data standards, messaging, data structures, and data recording, continues to be a significant barrier to an interoperable infrastructure.

The work on patient safety illustrated the importance of recording and distinguishing between pre-existing conditions and those acquired during hospital stay (and consequently the importance of developing "present on admission" flags), along with coding for secondary diagnoses. US Medicare took the lead on this – as of 2008, hospitals do not receive additional payment for cases in which one of the selected conditions was not present on admission, and are paid as if such secondary diagnoses (*i.e.* hospital acquired conditions) are not there.

Privacy

A natural by-product of existing clinical and administrative activity is an increasing array of rich data sources and datasets. Many such resources contain personally identifiable or potentially identifiable data. The increasing volume, complexity, and diversity of health care data and information systems, as well as approaches to identifying and linking datasets, pose significant problems for the future. Widespread use of personal health data outside of the primary care setting often occurs with commercial intent as employers, payers, and insurers seek to fulfill their business objectives. Furthermore, as EHRs continue to evolve and the adoption of health information technology increases, more health data will become available – this may also be accompanied by increased efforts to access and use these data for non-patient care purposes.

The public health dimension

Current ICT systems typically do not have thorough coverage of public health concepts and terms. ICD-9-CM is one of the more widely used terminologies because it is used for billing, but it captures relatively few of the clinical details that would be useful for surveillance. New concept-based public health vocabularies may need to be expanded or a controlled public health vocabulary developed.

An effort will be needed to expand on the clinical data elements being collected. This will require the identification of the essential data needs of various country level national agencies; identifying which kinds of data are needed at the population-level that could help ensure that they are collected at the point of care. Population health recognises that health is dependent upon multiple factors, including individual characteristics, the community, the environment, and a host of social and psychological factors, yet current EHR systems seldom capture data elements other than clinical ones.

Large volume of data – little information

Another issue is the capacity of public health agencies and population health researchers to cull data from EHRs. EHRs will annually generate billions of health events, prescriptions, test orders, laboratory and test results, and so forth in a typical medium-sized OECD country. New technologies will be needed for data storage, handling, and use. In order to utilise electronic patient records and electronic health records for population health monitoring and research, public health will need new technologies and methodologies that will enable it derive needed data in an appropriate form.

3.4. Improving health information systems and data infrastructures

International variations in completeness and quality of collected patient data restrict meaningful comparisons of health care systems. Furthermore, the lack of health data infrastructures is another limiting factor in quality indicator development. This is especially the case when one considers the lack of electronic health records, unique patient identifiers or linkage between databases. In order to secure quality of care, it is in the interest of all countries to monitor health status as well as quality of care indicators. For this, health and health care data collection needs to be organised in a systematic and efficient way, reconciling and linking data from different sources. As this involves issues of privacy and health care organisation legislation, improving data infrastructure needs political support from national and federal governments.

Improving health information systems and data infrastructures is feasible, while respecting legislative and patient privacy concerns. Valid ethical and legal concerns relating to data linkage and unique patient identifiers have implications relating to informed consent and the potential misuse of personal and population level data. However, these concerns can be addressed by developing robust procedures to safeguard anonymity and privacy. Data encryption methods and organisational procedures, along with informed and open public consultation all have their part to play in achieving this. The public may not be aware that the quality of their care is often compromised by both a lack of information and transparency. Public opinion therefore can serve as a powerful lever in moving these issues forward.

HCQI's subgroup expert panels continuously share updates on the development of their national, regional and organisational information systems, and data availability for all major domain indicators. For example, the subgroup on patient experiences has developed a set of principles for establishing national systems of patient experience measurement. The OECD ICT Project (see Box 3.3) provides advice in relation to the range of policy options, conditions and practices that can influence the implementation and adoption of ICTs. Such technical work is not going to make headlines in newspapers, but is absolutely essential if we wish to learn from the successes – and failures – of attempts to improve the quality of care in different countries.

Box 3.3. OECD Information and Communication Technologies Project

Despite the promise they hold out, implementing information and communication technologies (ICTs) in clinical care has proven to be a very difficult undertaking. More than a decade of efforts provide a picture of significant public investments, resulting in both notable successes and some highly publicised costly delays and failures. This has been accompanied by a failure to achieve widespread understanding among the general public and the medical profession of the benefits of electronic record keeping and information exchange.

With consistent cross-country information on these issues largely absent, the OECD has used lessons learned from case studies in Australia, Canada, the Netherlands, Spain, Sweden and the United States to identify the opportunities offered by ICTs and to analyse under what conditions these technologies are most likely to result in efficiency and quality-of-care improvements. The findings highlight a number of practices or approaches that could usefully be employed in efforts to improve and accelerate the adoption and use of these technologies.

For more information on the OECD ICT, see OECD (2010), *Improving Health Sector Efficiency: The Role of Information and Communication Technologies*, OECD Publishing, Paris.

3.5. Promoting the information agenda

This chapter addressed the key developments in national information infrastructures that are required to enhance and progress the development of nationally and internationally comparable indicators of care quality across health systems. Policy makers need to consider their current and anticipated investment in information systems and assess to whether it adequately meets future requirements.

For examples, some key issues to consider could relate to:

- *Efficiency:* the requirement of good information on quality is essential for developing and introducing value-based approaches to funding health care. As DRGs were fundamental to case-mix funding, clinical and care quality indicators are fundamental to P4P and bundled systems of payment for care.

- *Prevention:* balance of investment in population-based information systems (*e.g.* surveys) for primary prevention versus patient-based information systems for primary care (*e.g.* EPR).

- *Primary care:* strategies to develop national clinically-based primary care information systems useful for monitoring system level quality of care (*e.g.* standards for indicators built into the development plans).

Chapter 4

How Can Quality Indicators Be Used for Health System Improvement?

Using illustrative case studies taken from Belgium and Denmark, this chapter identifies the key touch points for quality improvement within health systems and discusses how health care quality indicators can be used proactively to improve quality.

This chapter addresses how quality indicators can be used to improve health system performance. Ensuring that quality indicators relate meaningfully to policy imperatives aimed at improving quality is central to achieving this.

In broad terms, there are four policy touch points in health systems that can influence the quality of care. These are: health system inputs health system design, monitoring mechanisms and improvement systems (see Table 4.1).

Table 4.1. How to improve quality of care

Policy type	Examples
Health system input (professionals, organisations, technologies)	Accreditation & certification of health care institutes Professional licensing & credentialing. Assessment and control of pharmaceutical products and medical devices
Health system design (allocation of responsibilities)	Accountability requirements, Quality Governance at the level of hospitals, primary care, social care. Quality as part of contracting and patient choice.
Monitoring (standards and information systems)	National standards and guidelines. Regulation on public reporting (policies towards registries, administrative databases, EHR and patient surveys). National audit studies
Improvement (incentive structures and [national] programmes)	Financial incentives such as pay for performance. National programmes on patient safety and quality improvement.

4.1. Health system inputs

Competent clinicians, high-performing hospitals and safe technologies are crucial health system inputs. All OECD countries have implemented various mechanisms to assure the quality of practising professionals. Examples are mandatory continuous (medical) education (CME), peer-review programmes and regular assessment of the performance of individual professionals. These mechanisms are related to regulation through licensing and credentialing. For example in the Netherlands all specialists are re-registered every four years. The re-registration process assesses the extent to which defined CME and peer review performance assessment requirements have been met. Quality measures are a prominent feature in ensuring this process takes place rigorously, impartially and transparently. For example, it is increasingly common for information used within the peer review process, particularly that which pertains to quality of care, to be shared in the public domain.

The quality of hospital care is similarly reassessed through periodic accreditation processes. The first accreditation programmes for hospitals stem from the United States (Joint Commission) and have spread widely to, for example, Canada, Australia, France, the United Kingdom and Spain. Accreditation programmes assess the compliance of hospitals with standards through site visits by trained accreditation teams. Increasingly hospitals have also to report on quality measures to the accreditation organisation in-between the site visits.

Specific medical technologies or services can also be the focus of quality assurance. Certification programmes, often based on ISO norms, are now routine in health care and sit alongside the regulation of the safety of pharmaceutical products and medical devices.

4.2.   Health system design

Health system design determines the responsibilities of various stakeholders in delivering quality. Roles and responsibilities for delivering quality can be assigned to professionals, management, payers (for example insurers or municipalities), governmental bodies, patients and the public. Irrespective of the nature or type of health care system, responsibilities for quality need to be allocated and performance relative to agreed quality thresholds must be transparent.

Incorporating quality into health system design raises important questions. How is it possible to achieve a reasonable balance between professional autonomy and accountability? To what extent are managers responsible for quality in the organisations they manage? How transparent should quality of care be to patients and the public? Can patients be held responsible for their quality of care? Are health care financiers responsible for the quality of the care they purchase? To what extent can government be held responsible for the quality of care?

In the main, countries have legislation in place that defines and demarcates responsibility and accountability for quality of care. For countries with largely regionalised health care systems (United States, Spain. Australia, Canada, Italy) general principles are set at a federal level and regional reports on quality of care help to compare regional performance. Invariably the development and use of quality indicators is part of the chosen governance models (Legido-Quigley and McKee, 2008; Spencer and Walshe, 2009; Jha and Epstein, 2010).

4.3.   Health system and services monitoring

Regional and national reports on quality of care are based on monitoring policies that deal with the actual measurement and reporting on quality of care. Monitoring needs to be based on a well-functioning national information infrastructure and the challenges in developing such a system have been described earlier in Chapter 3. As well as the use of international comparative data in these reports, Box 4.1 describes the Belgian approach to reporting on health systems at different levels.

The internet is increasingly used as an effective tool for the public release of information on quality of care. These public information portals are often part of an overall accountability and transparency agenda in countries that tend more towards market oriented health care systems aimed at increasing patient choice. Although evidence of the impact of this type of approach on patient choice is scare, public reporting of performance on quality does have "reputational" impact on professionals and institutions and, as such, can have an impact on the improvement of performance (Bevan *et al.*, 2010).

In addition, national standards and guidelines can help to calibrate the interpretation of these measures. The past 20 years have seen a rapid proliferation of national practice guidelines in health care. Initially, clinical guideline development was controlled almost exclusively by professionals and their associations with guidance often based on consensus amongst experts. Then, following heightened interest in the principles of evidence-based medicine in the late 1980s, the development of clinical guidelines became more formalised with inputs from experts, systematic literature reviews and meta-analyses of clinical trials.

Box 4.1. National performance reports in Belgium
Performance of the Belgian health care system: a first step towards assessment ...

In 2010, Belgium published a report assessing health care performance. In 2008, in line with the principles set out in the Tallinn Charter on health systems, the Belgian government committed itself to "promoting transparency and being accountable for health system performance through the publication of measurable results", including information on the quality of care. The report was produced under the responsibility of scientific bodies and the National Institute for Health and Disability Insurance (INAMI). Authorities with an interest in the areas of social affairs and public health – whether at regional, community or federal level – were also involved in the project.

Five main areas were considered in the analysis of the performance of the health system: quality, accessibility, efficiency, durability/continuity and fairness. The discussion paper established a list of 55 performance indicators. The choice of indicators was guided by pragmatism and priority was given to indicators considered valid by other countries' or indicators considered appropriate for use for international comparison purpose (the OECD publication *Health at a Glance* and the HCQI Project).

The report provided an opportunity for reflection on the optimisation and use of the databases available in Belgium. The policymakers consulted also stressed the value of having a joint tool, shared by the various authorities, that would validate international comparisons, assess health programmes, improve the performance of the health system and ensure accountability.

The Belgian authorities have agreed that the next report will be published by the end of December 2012.

Gradually other elements have been added to the guideline development process. These include, information on cost-effectiveness, patient's values, ethical concerns, barriers to implementation, resources and incentives required to implement guidelines in real life. This broadening of the guideline development process has brought with it increased involvement of stakeholders and enhanced ownership. Alongside profession-based programmes there are many national programmes (see *www.g-i-n.net/* website of Guidelines International Network).

Guidelines and standards can provide valuable benchmarks for setting quality thresholds. It is important therefore to design quality indicators with these thresholds in mind – in doing so, indicators are more likely resonate with quality imperatives and are more likely to be sensitive to quality breaches. Quality indicators derived from guidelines are usually structure- or process-based. Outcome indicators are less common but can be derived as long as the data required to construct the measures are clearly defined and systematically collected via, for example, specialty-specific registries.

Conversely, information on quality derived from indicators can be an important input to the guideline development process. In the future, information on actual quality performance should have similar import for guideline development as evidence from the international literature.

4.4. Health system improvement

Targets for improving the quality of care are increasingly used by countries. Apart from non-monetary incentives such as, the reputation of the provider, monetary incentives such as Pay-for-Performance schemes are used in the United States, United Kingdom and Korea (see also Section 1.6). National initiatives such as patient safety or quality improvement programmes are also examples of system-wide approach to improve quality. Many of these initiatives have been inspired by the US Institute for Health Care Improvement and safety programmes instigated by the WHO *www.who.int/patientsafety/en/*). National safety programmes are currently running in Australia, New Zealand, Germany, France, the United Kingdom and the United States.

Safety programmes can initiate new and important quality-related information collections *e.g.* risk registers and adverse event reporting. While these data are sensitive in nature, they are integral to gaining a comprehensive understanding of quality and, as such, should not be seen as separate or special. This also applies to secondary use of data, where disparate information streams can for example be linked together for purposes other than their original intended use *i.e.* quality monitoring. Important privacy and confidentiality issues arise from such applications. However, a sensible balance must also be struck between protecting the public interest on the one hand while ensuring that quality is robustly measured and improved on the other.

Aside from national programmes on patient safety and quality improvement, health care organisations have seen a rise in the introduction of service-industry quality models. Examples of these include the Baldrige model, the EFQM model and the Balanced Score Card. These models help organisations to develop systems that should aid performance management.

The quality strategies identified above are not intended to be exhaustive. The generic theme that runs through this chapter is that information that is collected to assess quality at the macrolevel should relate, where possible, to the quality information collected at the meso and microlevel. Ensuring that these strata are coherently linked will optimise consistency and congruency in data collection and will ensure that there is good resonance between overarching policy imperatives and local measurement practices.

Box 4.2 describes how in Denmark quality strategies are based on an information infrastructure that links performance data on micro, meso and macrolevel.

In conclusion, quality indicator work can contribute directly and indirectly to quality improvement strategies. Furthermore, the information that is gleaned from the use and interpretation of well constructed indicators is in itself an essential component effective policy development for quality improvement purposes.

Box 4.2. Documenting and improving quality in health care – an example from Denmark

The aim of the Danish National Indicator Project is to document and develop patient quality of care.

The other objectives of the project are to enhance: quality comparisons (benchmarking); quality judgments; options for priority setting; support for accountability; transparency of quality in health care. The initiative has been implemented in all clinical departments in Denmark. Participation is mandatory.

The Danish National Indicator Project was established in 2000 as a concerted action between the Ministry of Health, the National Board of Health, the Danish regions, the Danish Medical Association, the Danish Nursing Association, the Scientific Societies, the Association of Physiotherapists, and the Danish Association of Occupational Therapists. So far these organisations have prioritised eight diseases on the basis of most heavy DRG values (incidence and expenditure) in the Danish hospital services. The eight diseases are: Stroke, diabetes, hip fracture, schizophrenia, acute intestinal surgery, heart failure, chronic obstructive lung disease (COLD) and lung cancer.

From 2000 to 2008 evidence-based disease-specific quality indicators have been developed by multi-professional clinicians appointed by the respective scientific societies.

To secure the comparability of data, prognostic factors are used to adjust for case mix. It is hereby possible to evaluate whether favourable or unfavourable outcomes are due to the health care system or due to conditions over which the health care system has no influence. Clinicians and managers received continuous feedback of results after a professional process of analysis, interpretation, and evaluation, the data are released publicly.

The experiences from 2000 to 2008 indicate that the quality of care related to the areas covered improve over time and that performance and outcome measurement can be used to drive quality improvement.

Some results from the Danish National Indicator Project

The table below shows the results related to evidence-based stroke indicators in the Danish National Indicator Project. Improvements are seen for all indicators in the period 2003-08.

Stroke indicators and results from the Danish National Indicator Project in 2003 and 2008

Indicator	2008	2003
Proportion of patients admitted to a stroke unit	91 (90-91)	77 (76-78)
Antiplatelet Therapy: Proportion of patients with acute ischemic stroke without atrial fibrillation, where platelet inhibitor treatment is not contraindicated, treated with platelet inhibitor	87 (86-88)	69 (68-71)
Oral anticoagulant therapy: Proportion of patients treated with anticoagulants	73 (70-76)	45 (42-49)
Proportion of patients who undergo a CT/MRI scan	67 (66-68)	43 (41-44)
Proportion of patients assessed by a physiotherapist	73 (72-73)	42 (40-43)
Proportion of patients assessed by an occupational therapist	70 (69-71)	35 (34-36)
Proportion of patients who have their nutritional status evaluated	68 (67-69)	43 (41-44)
30-days mortality	10 (10-11)	12 (11-12)

Figure A. Mortality rates by treatment

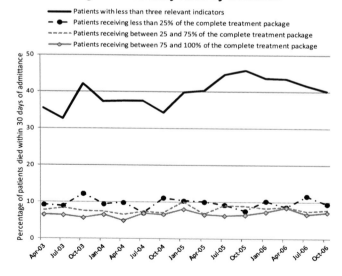

Figure A describes a dose response correlation between proportion of interventions that patients with stroke have received and 30-day mortality rate (2003-07) in the Danish National Indicator Project.

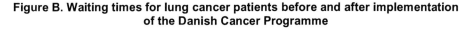

Figure B. Waiting times for lung cancer patients before and after implementation of the Danish Cancer Programme

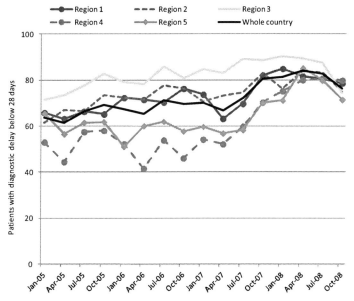

Figure B describes waiting times for lung cancer patients' examinations before and after implementation of cancer programme in the Danish Health Care System. The Danish Cancer programmes were introduced in the Danish Health Care System in 2007.

Bibliography

Bevan, G., J. Helderman and D. Wilsford (2010), "Changing Choices in Health Care: Implications for Equity, Efficiency and Cost", *Health Economics, Policy and Law*, Vol. 5, No. 3, pp. 251-267.

Jha, A. and A. Epstein (2010), "Hospital Governance and the Quality of Care", *Health Affairs*, pp. 182-187.

Legido-Quigley, H. and M.W. McKee (2008), "How Can Quality of Health Care Be Safeguarded Across the European Union?", *British Medical Journal*, Vol. 26, No. 336(7650), pp. 920-923.

Spencer, E. and K. Walshe (2009), "National Quality Improvement Policies and Strategies in European Healthcare Systems", *Quality and Safety in Health Care*, Vol. 18, Suppl. 1, pp. i22-27.

Chapter 5

Conclusions and Recommendations

Health care systems today face tremendous challenges: complex care needs and care processes, increased health care demands especially for chronic conditions and perhaps most importantly, an economic landscape where health care systems will have to achieve more for less. Quality has a fundamental bearing on all these challenges. Poor quality of care undermines every goal of modern health systems. It results in poor patient satisfaction, excess morbidity and premature mortality, and increased health costs.

In this report we have described why information on health care quality is important and how it can be used to improve health care. The report highlights examples drawn from around the world that illustrate how quality improvement initiatives can be implemented in real health system settings. Despite these examples, there is clearly much work to be done and quality improvement is not amenable to a "one size fits all" solution. That said, the experience gained from international experts and quality initiatives in one country after another point to a number of generalisable learning points. These are set out in the recommendations below:

Recommendations to improve measurement and use of quality of care indicators

Recommendations regarding the measurement of health care quality indicators

- Develop legislation that strikes a balance between privacy and data-protection concerns on the one hand and the need for reliable and valid information for quality-led governance on the other.

- Fully exploit the potential of (national) registries and administrative databases for measuring quality of care – particularly through the implementation of unique patient identifiers, secondary diagnostic coding and present-on-admission flags (*i.e.* to facilitate the distinction between quality issues that are the responsibility of hospital or others).

- Implement the comprehensive use of electronic health records for measuring quality of care as part of population-based statistics.

- Establish national systems to collect longitudinal information on patient experience.

Recommendations regarding the application of Health Care Quality Indicators

- Ensure that common quality indicators are used when considering quality improvement at macro, meso and microlevels.

- Assure consistency and linkage of quality measurement efforts with (national) quality policies on health system input (professionals, hospitals, technologies) health system design (distribution of responsibilities for quality and accountability), monitoring (standards, guidelines and information-infrastructure) and health system improvement (national quality and safety programmes and quality incentives).

- Seek examples of good quality improvement practice from other countries, and identify what and how that learning can be applied locally.

This report has illustrated that quality can be measured and quality indicators can be actively used to improve performance. Better national information infrastructures and advice linking on quality indicators to national quality strategies and policies are paramount to improving value in health care.

OECD PUBLISHING, 2, rue André-Pascal, 75775 PARIS CEDEX 16
PRINTED IN FRANCE
(81 2010 19 1 P) ISSN 2074-3181 – No. 57641 2010